C.3

DATE DUE

SEP 2 4	
JAN 0 2 1996	APR 5 1996
H836429	
OCT 2 8 1999	

PRINTED IN U.S.A.

GAYLORD

Assessing Dangerousness

Interpersonal Violence:
The Practice Series
Jon R. Conte, Series Editor

Interpersonal Violence: The Practice Series is devoted to mental health, social service, and allied professionals who confront daily the problem of interpersonal violence. It is hoped that the knowledge, professional experience, and high standards of practice offered by the authors of these volumes may lead to the end of interpersonal violence.

In this series...

Assessing Dangerousness

Violence by Sexual Offenders, Batterers, and Child Abusers

edited by
Jacquelyn C. Campbell

Interpersonal Violence:
The Practice Series

SAGE Publications
International Educational and Professional Publisher
Thousand Oaks   London   New Delhi

For information address:

SAGE Publications, Inc.
2455 Teller Road
Thousand Oaks, California 91320

SAGE Publications Ltd.
6 Bonhill Street
London EC2A 4PU
United Kingdom

SAGE Publications India Pvt. Ltd.
M-32 Market
Greater Kailash I
New Delhi 110 048 India

Printed in the United States of America

Library of Congress Cataloging-in-Publication Data

Main entry under title:

Assessing dangerousness: Violence by sexual offenders, batterers, and child abusers / edited by Jacquelyn C. Campbell.
    p.   cm.—(Interpersonal violence: The practice series; vol. 8)
  Includes bibliographical references and indexes.
  ISBN 0-8039-3746-6.—ISBN 0-8039-3747-4 (pbk.)
  1. Violence—Forecasting. 2. Family violence—Forecasting.
3. Sex crimes—Forecasting. I. Campbell, Jacquelyn C. II. Series:
Interpersonal violence; v. 8.
RC569.5.V55A87 1995
616.85′82′00112—dc20
                                   94-31772

95 96 97 98 99 10 9 8 7 6 5 4 3 2 1

Sage Production Editor: Yvonne Könneker

Contents

Preface

All of us, the contributors to this volume, have been in clinical situations in which we have been asked to determine how violent an individual is likely to be, how much danger his or her possible victim is actually in. In courts, clinics, conference rooms, battered women's shelters, hospital emergency rooms, research settings, and private offices, we have faced the difficult problem of prediction. And we have been acutely aware of how this issue has profound implications, intersecting our clinical judgments, our advocacy agendas, and our ethical responsibilities. The contributors are all clinicians to a certain extent, and we have a proud respect for the work that practitioners are doing in the family violence and sexual assault fields. But each of us has also added a research involvement to his or her clinical base. Thus we are trying to add what we know from our research to the difficult problem of clinical prediction of violence in situations of child and wife abuse and sexual violence. We have tried to be helpful to all of us—clinicians and researchers in various combinations of history and roles—in this volume. We offer you our summary of the research in this area, as well as the instruments that may be helpful and the criteria by which to judge them. To this, you will add your own clinical expertise.

I would like to thank all of the contributors for their responsiveness to reviews, their patience with the process, and their collective wisdom and commitment to these issues. Especially I would like to thank Jon Conte for his leadership in creating these volumes and in the field of interpersonal violence. The staff at Sage have also been extremely helpful in this production and have done an incredible service to all of us in so skillfully disseminating all of our research and practice insights in this field. Finally, I would like to acknowledge the unfailing help and support of my research staff, especially Cheryl Smith, Mary Cardwell, Ruth Ann Belknap, Chris Miller, Patricia Price, Nancy O'Connor, and Diane Lancaster. And always to my parents, Christy, Brad, and Reg, my thanks and love.

JACQUELYN C. CAMPBELL

1

Prediction of Intentional Interpersonal Violence: An Introduction

Barbara J. Limandri
Daniel J. Sheridan

Clinicians who work in interpersonal violence are asked frequently to make predictions about violent behavior. Most notably, clinicians are asked by law enforcement personnel, child and elder protective services workers, and civil and criminal court officials to predict the likelihood of future violence by alleged and/or convicted family violence and sexual assault perpetrators. These assessments of "dangerousness" serve the primary function of controlling behavior by punishment, treatment, or confinement (Cleveland, Mulvey, Appelbaum, & Lidz, 1989; Gondolf, Mulvey, & Lidz, 1990; Gottfredson & Gottfredson, 1988) and seek to prevent the occurrence of repeated violence. In this chapter we review what generally is known about the prediction of violent behavior in clinical settings and then discuss implications for the prediction of interpersonal violence. Succeeding chapters address the specific variables involved in the prediction of child abuse and neglect, sexual violence, and heterosexual spousal abuse. This volume represents the most current research, trends, and professional viewpoints regarding the prediction of interpersonal violence. Although the prediction of interpersonal violence is in its infancy, it is an area of utmost importance. Many clinicians are confronted with these issues on a daily basis. Consider the following scenario.

A Clinical Reality: Hospital-Based Intervention

8:00 a.m.: You are paged to the intensive care unit to see a critically injured patient just admitted from the emergency department (ED). The woman has multiple fractures to her face, bruises to her chest and back, and a partially ruptured spleen. She tells you that 2 days ago her husband struck her with a board and kicked her multiple times. He would not let her seek medical care. She thinks that earlier today she must have passed out at home from internal bleeding. She was driven to the ED by her husband, who then left the hospital. She tells you that her husband has a permit to carry a concealed weapon and that he frequently has threatened to kill her and the children if she ever tried to leave the relationship. She asks, "Will my husband beat me again? Could he kill me or my kids?"

8:25 a.m.: The hospital administrator pages you and wants to know whether this patient's husband poses a risk of harm to other patients, staff, or visitors.

8:50 a.m.: You are paged by a child protective services department investigator. She tells you she has been investigating this family because of a recent child abuse allegation filed by the school. The children did not arrive at school this morning, and they are not at home. She thinks they may be with their father. She asks you whether you think the children are at risk of abuse and whether the mother knows of their whereabouts.

9:00 a.m.: You are paged by the ED staff to see another patient, a woman who was just raped and then shot in the hip by her former husband. On the basis of the patient's initial history, the ED staff has fears that he may come to the hospital to "finish what he started." They ask whether you think this man is capable of coming to the ED to kill his former wife.

9:05 a.m.: You are paged by the prosecuting attorney's office to confirm that you will testify in court around 11:00 a.m. on a case from several months ago.

❑ Predictive Settings

The above scenario is a real-life example of a day in the life of a clinician who works with domestic and sexual violence survivors in crisis. As illustrated, the clinician is called on repeatedly to make assessments and predictions of risk, often after obtaining only a cursory history of the violent behavior and without any direct contact with the alleged perpetrator. Clinicians in acute incident settings (e.g., hospital workers, field investigators, hot-line workers) are especially pressed for time. In these instances

> *The clinician is called on repeatedly to make assessments and predictions of risk.*

"predictions" are likely to be "best guesses" based on the clinician's intuition, knowledge, experience, and biases.

Typically this initial prediction, or assessment of risk, will be revisited several times and in a number of settings. In the criminal justice system, documentation and/or testimony regarding the defendant's propensity for violence may influence a variety of judicial outcomes. For example, the court may ask the clinician to predict the likelihood of future violence when sentencing a convicted offender. The expert opinion of the clinician may significantly affect sentence length. Likewise such testimony may influence the eligibility of convicted offenders to participate in new, innovative, deferred sentencing programs or other forms of alternative dispensation that now are being developed. In family court clinicians' predictions of future violence may influence the court's ruling on a protection from abuse order or on issues of child custody and protection. Clearly the clinician's assessment of dangerousness can be an enormously valuable resource.

This value highlights the need for the development of accurate and reliable models for the prediction of interpersonal violence.

❏ Clinically Based Prediction Models

The prediction of interpersonal violence demands the use of psychometrically sound measurements and an understanding of such tools' limitations. Research in clinical decision making (Benner, 1984; Harbison, 1991; Schon, 1983a) identifies three major models for prediction: (a) the linear, rationalist model, (b) the hypothetico-deductive model, and (c) the risk assessment model (Gottfredson & Gottfredson, 1988). Depending on the goal of the assessment, the clinician may use aspects of one or more of these models.

LINEAR MODEL

Because prediction has such significant forensic implications, clinicians may use a linear model, including a decision tree or critical pathway, to guide them when making decisions that have legal ramifications. For example, Gross, Southard, Lamb, and Weinberger (1987) propose seven steps to follow when a client makes suggestive threats (see Figure 1.1).

Step 1 is to clarify the threat. Many clients make vague comments that may or may not indicate a real danger. Thus the clinician must take the time to fully explore intent. For example, after an acute beating, a battered woman may state that she wishes someone would "blow his [the abuser's] brains out." In this case the clinician needs to ask the client directly whether she intends to kill her abuser. This client simply may be expressing her anger. Further inquiry might reveal that she does not own or have access to a firearm. In the above case the risk factor for retaliatory violence is low, especially when compared with the client who tells the clinician that she would like to kill her abuser and has borrowed her brother's loaded handgun.

Thus, if there is a clear threat, Step 2 is to assess its lethality, as well as the likelihood of the person acting on the threat. As with suicidal thoughts, not all "threats" pose a true danger or can be enacted. The

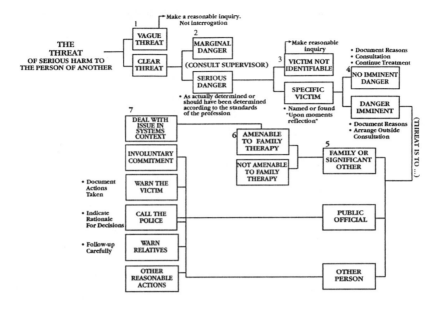

Figure 1.1. Decision Tree for Assessing Interpersonal Violence

SOURCE: Gross et al. (1987). Assessing dangerousness and responding appropriately: *Hedlund* expands the clinician's liability established by *Tarasoff*. *Journal of Clinical Psychiatry, 48*(1), 9-12. Copyright © 1987, Physicians Postgraduate Press. Reprinted by permission.

incarcerated client may verbalize specific threats of violence against someone outside of prison but have no means to carry through on the threats.

If there is evidence of danger, Step 3 is to identify a specific, intended victim. In family violence and family sexual assault cases, it is easy to identify intended victims. The violence is seldom random, even within homes in which multiple members reside. The clinician working with a client who is verbalizing concerns about physically and/or sexually assaulting a stranger may find it more difficult to identify a specific victim (by name). However, the clinician can ask the client to indicate the intended victim's gender and any specific victim characteristics.

If the client can name the intended victim or specifics about the type of victim who will be sought, the threat of harm is imminent

(Step 4). At this point the clinician needs to consider his or her duty to warn the specified victim. For more detail the reader is referred to material on the Tarasoff decisions (*Tarasoff v. Regents of the University of California*, 1974, 1976).

The clinician also must take into account the client's relationship to the intended victim (Step 5). If the intended victim is a family member, rather than a political figure, the clinician may employ different preventive and treatment strategies.

Step 6 requires the clinician to decide whether a family therapy intervention would be suitable. For example, if the family violence is ongoing, family therapy may impose greater danger to the potential victim or victims.

Finally, Step 7 requires the clinician to consider whether civil commitment or involuntary hospitalization would provide the greatest good to the client and potential victim or victims. At the completion of Step 7, the clinician needs to follow up on the results of the decisions made and may need to recycle through the decision tree at a later date.

The strength of the linear model is that it provides relatively clear direction for the clinician, as well as a "logical" argument for the decision. Using the linear model, the clinician approaches problem solving with some notion of probability. He or she weighs outcomes according to objective standards or theory. The weakness of this model is also its objectivity; contextually relevant information is given little consideration. In other words, factors such as treatment outcomes, social support, and stabilization of stress are not considered in making the prediction. The decision is driven by formula, more than by the specifics of the actual situation.

HYPOTHETICO-DEDUCTIVE MODEL

By contrast, the hypothetico-deductive model tends to be relational and complex in assessing factors that influence clinical decisions. As with the linear model, the clinician weighs different factors, but the problem is considered more in context. In addition, past experiences with similar situations provide the clinician with patterns of cues to consider and ways to categorize the cues. In considering all of the information in the current situation, the expert is searching for a "pivotal cue" to frame all of the cues and to link with extensive theoretical and experiential knowledge (Regan-Kubinski, 1991; Schon, 1983b). After the clinician has focused his or her questioning and assessment, he or she begins to search specifically for additional cues relevant to violence and protectiveness. In clustering the cues, the expert continually loops back to the context of the specific client and to the overall context of the community in which the situation is occurring. Finally, the clinician arranges the cues into some hypotheses and reviews the hypotheses for completeness. He or she may seek additional cues to complete the picture if necessary. The hypotheses then are tested for confirmation or refutation, and a final decision is made. The following case example illustrates this process:

> While tightly clenching his fists, a young man tells his high school counselor that his grades plummeted because his girlfriend, whom he refers to in sexually derogatory terms, broke off their relationship. The counselor knows that this student has a history of frequent alcohol abuse and fighting on school grounds. The young man's father is in the Navy on an extended overseas assignment. The mother reports that her son refuses to accept her authority and that he has become difficult to manage in the absence of the father.

Using the hypothetico-deductive model, the clinician first focuses on the cues of anger, age, rejection by the girlfriend, and alcohol abuse, reaching the pivotal cue of "potential for dangerousness." The counselor also hypothesizes that the young man may be depressed, feeling out of control, and feeling abandoned, all of which would contribute to his potential for violence. In addition, the counselor considers such cues as the school's location in east Los Angeles and the school's climate after the 1992 riots, reports of several similar situations with the other young men in the school, and reports that the girls in the school have been complaining about violence by the boys. The counselor reaches the judgment that not only is this young man potentially dangerous but also there may be a systemic problem in the school and community. Thus the immediate plan is to confront the young man's anger and to recommend some structured physical activity. The counselor also determines that the girlfriend has different classes from the boyfriend and that the possibility of contact that day is slight. The young man contracts to stay away from the girl-friend and not harm her. To meet the community problem recognized by this model, the counselor consults with his female colleague and together they plan a special assembly on the topic of dating violence. They also set up gender-segregated peer groups to discuss violence in the community and within dating relationships.

RISK ASSESSMENT MODEL

A major reason for poor predictive accuracy of interpersonal violence is the assumption that violence is dichotomous and single dimensional (Gottfredson & Gottfredson, 1988). Instead of a binary notion of violence, Gottfredson and Gottfredson propose a risk-to-stakes matrix wherein the seriousness of the action is weighed with the likelihood of repetition. Seriousness permits the assessor to consider types of harm possible across a multitude of variables. Alcohol and drug use, for example, might influence the likelihood of harm, as well might a history of violence. By means of the risk assessment model, clinicians can provide assessments of risk factors or risk markers that may contribute to violence. Such a model incorporates the social and political climate, as well as the individual's internal climate. The risk assessment model permits clinicians to weigh both the environmental and personal factors present in any given situation. The following case demonstrates this model:

> Convicted of felony assault on his former girlfriend, a 28-year-old male with a history of alcoholism is up for parole after serving half of a 12-month sentence. While in prison, he completed extensive alcohol treatment and anger management programs. On release from jail he intends to live with his mother. As the clinician, it would be imperative to know that his mother lives less than a block from the former girlfriend and that living in the mother's home are several alcoholic siblings.

Releasing this man into his mother's home, into close contact with alcoholic siblings, places him at high risk for drinking. Because his mother lives so close to his former girlfriend, further abuse is also quite possible. Instead of recommending against parole, the clinician may advise that parole be contingent on housing arrangements that do not place the offender in such close contact with either alcohol or his prior victim.

The three clinical decision-making models discussed above are distinct, but not necessarily exclusive, means for deciding on interventions. In courtrooms linear decision routes are much easier to substantiate. However, decisions are rarely so clear-cut in the clinical arena. Therefore clinicians need to be adept in approaching (or at least justifying) these decisions from multiple perspectives.

❏ Predictive Reliability and Validity

The accuracy (validity) and consistency (reliability) of predicting dangerousness and violence depends on several factors. In general, using statistical probability, the more infrequent the event, the more difficult it is to predict (Lambert, Cartor, & Walker, 1988). For example, Steadman (1986) notes that homicide in the United States occurs at a base rate of 9 in 100,000, whereas family violence occurs at a base rate of 16,000 in 100,000. Accordingly, predictions of homi-

Family violence occurs at a base rate of 16,000 in 100,000.

cide are less likely to be accurate than predictions of family violence.

The accuracy, or "validity," of such a prediction may be influenced by a number of factors: the type of violence (e.g., physical assault, intimidation, suicide, property damage); the actors or participants (e.g., strangers, intimates, acquaintances); the psychological status of the perpetrators (e.g., people who are mentally ill, criminals, socially deviant, or ordinary); and the time period of the prediction (e.g., acute or chronic danger).

The succeeding chapters discuss in greater depth problems with assessment measures and predictor variables. It is clear, however, that assessments of risk and danger are improved when appropriately administered, psychometrically sound abuse assessment scales are coupled with specific demographic characteristics, clinical judgments, and context specific factors (e.g., stress measurements, locus of control measurements, social support).

❏ Poor Record of Past Predictions

Mental health professionals, in general, have a poor track record of validly predicting violence among the mentally ill (Convit, Jaeger, Lin, Meisner, & Volavka, 1988; Gondolf et al., 1990; McNeil, Binder, & Greenfield, 1988; Miller & Morris, 1988). Although an assessment of danger to self and/or others is a basic element of involuntary psychiatric treatment, individual psychiatrists have not been very successful in accurately predicting this danger (Beigel, Barren, & Harding, 1984; McNeil et al., 1988; Meloy, 1987; Steadman & Morrissey, 1982).

However, a consensus by multiple evaluators has higher predictive accuracy than when evaluators disagree (Werner, Rose, & Yesavage, 1990). When clinicians consult with each other (e.g., multidisciplinary review boards), they are able to pool their diverse knowledge and expertise in reaching a consensus. The social worker, psychologist, advanced nurse clinician, psychiatrist, counselor, and parole officer have very different perspectives; together they form a more complete gestalt.

We also are learning that predictions can be made more accurately when evaluators take into account such interactive factors as gender, marital state, concomitant use of disinhibiting agents, and availability of victims and weapons (Meloy, 1987; Segal, Watson, Goldfinger, & Averbuck, 1988). Although static predictors (e.g., age, gender, prior history) cannot be changed by intervention, dynamic predictors (e.g., perpetration attitudes and beliefs, probationary supervision) can be the focus of intervention, and risk may be reduced.

PREDICTIVE FACTORS

History of Violence. Research into the prediction of interpersonal violence consistently shows that a history of violence is one of the best predictors of future violence (Convit et al., 1988; Janofsky, Spears, & Neubauer, 1988; Lewis, Lovely, Yeager, & Femina, 1989; McNeil et al., 1988). For example, Blomhoff, Seim, and Friis (1990) used medical records in an effort to distinguish between violent and nonviolent patients at the time of admission to a psychiatric hospital. *Violence* was defined as any incident of physical aggression specifically directed at another person. The most significant factor between the two groups was previous violence ($p < .0001$).

In a similar study that used matched samples, Convit et al. (1988) noted that a self-reported history of violent crimes was the most salient risk factor. Likewise Monahan (1981, 1984) identified prior convictions or prior violent incidents as consistent predictors of further violence and homicide. Thus clinical predictions of violence will be made more accurately when the past history of violence is taken under serious consideration.

Mental Illness. Mental health clinicians must predict dangerousness as a requirement for emergency civil commitment, but mental health workers historically have a poor rate of predictive accuracy. At best, the accuracy rate remains around 40% (Menzies, Webster, & Sepejak, 1985). Because of (or in spite of) these poor predictive accuracy rates, there is great internal and external pressure on the mental health profession to develop more effective means of identifying patients who are likely to be violent because of their illness.

One of the most problematic aspects of the research on violence among psychiatric patients is the criteria used to identify "violent" acts and "violent" people. For example, psychiatric patients traditionally are assessed for danger to self and/or danger to others. As a result, suicide and self-mutilation may be included in the research, confusing the picture. Likewise the patient may demonstrate very different patterns of violent behavior when hospitalized (Holcomb & Ahr, 1988; Myers & Dunner, 1984) simply because of treatment and confinement. Because the severe mental illnesses (e.g., schizophrenia, bipolar disorder) are relapsing ones, violence is a greater factor in times of decompensation and psychosis than during stabilization (Craig, 1982; Krakowski, Jaeger, & Volavka, 1988; Tardiff & Sweillman, 1982).

Specific diagnostic groups that demonstrate the highest percent-ages of violent behaviors are substance abuse (alone), substance abuse with another psychiatric diagnosis, and personality disorders (Drummond, Sparr, & Gordon, 1989). Patients assigned multiple psychiatric diagnoses seem to demonstrate even higher percentages of violent acts; 22.36% of those with three or more concurrent psychiatric diagnoses reported violent behaviors, compared with 2.05% of those without a diagnosis (Swanson, Holzer, Ganju, & Jono, 1990).

To explore the prevalence of violence and its correlation with mental illness, the National Institute of Mental Health sponsored a representative, multicity study of about 10,000 psychiatrically treated and untreated people (Robins & Regier, 1991). Further analyzing these data, Swanson et al. (1990) found:

a five times higher prevalence of violence among those with an Axis I psychiatric diagnosis

that persons with severe mental illness (schizophrenia, major depression, manic and bipolar disorder) have similar rates of violence (11% to 12.7%)

that alcoholics had 12 times higher rates of violence

that drug users had 16 times higher rates of violence than nonalcoholics or nondrug users

Controlling for demographic and diagnostic factors, a profile for violence would include young, poor men with a history of substance abuse and/or severe mental illness (Swanson & Holzer, 1991).

Some behaviors that appear to be associated with mental illness are also common among people who exhibit dangerous behaviors. Using the Brief Psychiatric Rate Scale, various mental health profes-sionals found that patients who consistently showed conceptual disorganization, threatening mannerisms and posturing, grandiosity, hostility, suspiciousness, and excitement were more likely to be violent than patients who did not demonstrate these behaviors (Werner et al., 1990). Only one study examined specifically the perpetration of domestic violence by the psychiatric patients. In a study done in Sweden, Lindquist and Allebeck (1989) identified 38 patients with schizophrenia (from hospital records for 644 patients) who had committed 71 violent offenses; 11 of those acts were directed specifically against family members, and there was a significant history of family discord.

Substance Abuse. Although alcohol and/or drug use is cited frequently as the cause of interpersonal violence, most research simply describes a co-occurrence of alcohol and other substances with incidents of violence (Dobash & Dobash, 1979; Frieze & Schafer, 1984; Goodman, Mercy, & Loya, 1986; Goodman, Mercy, & Rosenberg, 1986; Lenke, 1982; Norton & Morgan, 1989a, 1989b, 1989c). Studies document the strong relationship between drug/alcohol blood levels and homicide, assault, and the use of handguns in crimes, but other important factors must be considered when proposing a causal relationship between substance abuse and violence.

For example, predrinking expectations seem to be most highly correlated with postdrinking behaviors (George, Dermen, & Nochajski, 1989). That is, if the drinker expects to be disinhibited and believes it is acceptable to be aggressive when intoxicated, the drinker is more likely to act on these beliefs after drinking. Drug abuse seems to be correlated similarly with domestic violence. Roberts (1988) found that 70.5% of abusers were under the influence of drugs and/or alcohol, with 32% using drugs only and 22% combining alcohol and drugs. Battering also seems to be more severe when alcohol and drugs are used in combination. According to Browne (1987), about 30% of abusers killed by their victims used street drugs every day or several times per week. Frequent street drug use also has been found to be a correlate of homicide of battered women.

Several classes of drugs biochemically and behaviorally produce very different effects. Among people with schizophrenia who committed violent offenses, there seems to be no preference for a particular drug, be it an amphetamine, opiate, cannabis, or solvent (Lindquist & Allebeck, 1989). More laboratory-focused studies, however, have identified marijuana, cocaine, and amphetamines as having a much stronger effect on aggressiveness and impulsivity than do alcohol, opioids, tranquilizers, barbiturates, hallucinogens, or inhalants (Fishbein, Lozovosky, & Jaffe, 1989; Jaffe, 1985). Abusive male partners were more likely to use marijuana and/or cocaine than nonabusive male partners (Amaro, Fried, Cabral, & Zuckerman, 1990).

Demographics. The literature about interpersonal violence tends to be gender-specific, depending on discussions about perpetrators or about victims. For example, many of the studies seeking to identify factors related to delinquency and violence have looked only at boys' behaviors (Josephson, 1987; Lewis et al., 1989; Mulvey & Reppucci, 1988). Therefore the research provides a limited perspective on the precursors to interpersonal violence. The girls (like the delinquent boys) also may have witnessed violence in their homes and watched violent television. Instead of presenting themselves as delinquents or as violent adult criminals, the females may be presenting themselves to mental health agencies for treatment of depression or other emotional distress.

Furthermore most research into domestic violence has been based on the heterosexual model of men abusing women. Little is known about gay and lesbian abuse. Assessment and predictive strategies developed in response to heterosexual intimate violence may not be as predictive with gay and lesbian intimate violence.

Research on the effects of childhood experiences on later aggression is inconclusive. In their review of police records, Lewis et al. (1989) found that juvenile violence was not sufficient explanation for violent criminal behavior as an adult. Instead they found it to be an interaction between a history of abuse and/or family violence and the cognitive, psychiatric, and neurological impairments of the child.

Other studies have tried to determine any link between divorce and later aggression and violence. In an extensive study of 528 university students, Billingham and Gilbert (1990) found that children of divorced parents had no greater incidence of dating violence than did children of intact families. Gender, likewise, made no significant difference, although males were more likely than females to have difficulty in relationships. This study used the Conflict Tactics Scale (CTS), which assesses for verbal as well as physical aggression. Likewise homicide shows no significant correlation with birth rate, unemployment, or divorce rates (Lester, 1987).

ETHICAL CONSIDERATIONS

Although the empirical study of the prediction of interpersonal violence is important, a number of moral and ethical issues should be considered. The clinician who must render an assessment of the probability of future violence has a responsibility to weigh several ethical issues; he or she must consider not only the social injustice of violence perpetrated against citizens but also the perpetrators' individual rights to autonomy and freedom. When do societal rights supersede individual rights, or one person's rights supersede another's?

An ongoing concern is the question of using mental health interventions as a form of social control versus as a way to alleviate emotional and psychological distress. When the clinician recommends commitment of an individual judged to be "dangerous," is the purpose of the action to help or control the perpetrator? If social control is the purpose, what treatment is appropriate—negative reinforcement, aversive therapy, psychotropic medications, or supportive and/or confrontive psychotherapy? Is informed consent necessary for social control, and is such consent even possible within a coercive environment?

Another problematic issue regarding the prediction of interpersonal violence is the potential for disguised or unconscious racism and classism. We know that more people of color than white people are incarcerated for violent crimes. Race, ethnicity, and class have a way of unmindfully influencing clinical judgment. Is it possible for the clinician to remain "objective" when making an assessment of dangerousness? Will the clinician be influenced by his or her identification with the victim or the offender?

When making predictions that influence the decision to incarcerate or release an alleged perpetrator, the clinician is balancing many factors that might contribute to a false positive error (the person is predicted to be more dangerous than he or she actually is). Although false positives may better protect society, they unfairly restrict the civil liberties of the offender.

❏ **Fact or Fantasy**

A common assumption that guides the practice of many family violence and sexual assault clinicians is that, for the most part, the perpetrators of these violent acts are not mentally ill. We already know that predicting dangerousness among the *mentally ill* is only marginally accurate (Gondolf et al., 1990; McNeil et al., 1988; Miller & Morris, 1988); is it fantasy to believe that we can develop criteria by which to predict family violence and sexual assaultive behaviors among those viewed as *normal*?

The court system looks to psychological and medical experts for judgments of an individual's potential for violence. The police bring individuals suspected of being dangerous to the emergency department to be diagnosed and to be "fixed." Women frequently ask clinicians, "How can I tell if my boyfriend (husband) is going to abuse me?" Women ask, "Is there a way to tell ahead of time if some guy is going to rape me on a date?" A child will ask, "Is Mommy or Daddy going to hurt me again?" Parents demand assurances that people who care for their children are not going to become physically or sexually abusive.

Whether or not we participate in formal research to test the predictive properties of a particular instrument or assessment method, all clinicians make predictions about dangerousness. It can be argued that it is not possible to truly refrain from making "predictions." These predictions may be based on such factors as past behaviors, clinical risk factors/risk markers, similar behaviors that have been observed in others, clinical evaluation of the alleged offender, and/or on prediction instruments.

Some clinicians underpredict the potential for danger, while others overpredict.

Some clinicians underpredict the potential for danger, while others overpredict. To underpredict the risk of further violence is to potentially place the client at risk of being killed or seriously hurt. When the clinician consistently overpredicts the potential for danger, the client may lose trust in the clinician's ability to identify a dangerous situation. The client may choose to ignore future predictions, again being placed in a vulnerable position. However, to overpredict the potential dangerousness of an identified abuser may be to participate in a process that unjustly incarcerates, labels, and/or blames a person for past behaviors. The difficult task for the clinician is to make a judgment between the two extremes. Obviously there are no easy answers.

Assessing dangerousness for further violence by sexual offenders, batterers, and child abusers is in its infancy. The following chapters explore the most current research, trends, and professional viewpoints regarding the prediction of interpersonal violence.

❏ References

Amaro, H., Fried, L. E., Cabral, H., & Zuckerman, B. (1990). Violence during pregnancy and substance use. *American Journal of Public Health, 80*(5), 575-579.

Beigel, A., Barren, M. R., & Harding, T. W. (1984). The paradoxical impact of a commitment statute on prediction of dangerousness. *American Journal of Psychiatry, 141*(3), 373-377.

Benner, P. (1984). *From novice to expert: Excellence and power in clinical nursing practice.* Reading, MA: Addison-Wesley.

Billingham, R. E., & Gilbert, K. R. (1990). Parental divorce during childhood and use of violence in dating relationships. *Psychological Reports, 66,* 1003-1009.

Blomhoff, S., Seim, S., & Friis, S. (1990). Can prediction of violence among psychiatric inpatients be improved? *Hospital and Community Psychiatry, 41*(7), 771-775.

Browne, A. (1987). *When battered women kill.* New York: Free Press.

Cleveland, S., Mulvey, E. P., Appelbaum, P. S., & Lidz, C. W. (1989). Do dangerousness-oriented commitment laws restrict hospitalization of patients who need treatment? A test. *Hospital and Community Psychiatry, 40*(3), 266-271.

Convit, A., Jaeger, J., Lin, S. P., Meisner, M., & Volavka, J. (1988). Predicting assaultiveness in psychiatric inpatients: A pilot study. *Hospital and Community Psychiatry, 39*(4), 429-434.

Craig, T. J. (1982). An epidemiological study of problems associated with violence among psychiatric inpatients. *American Journal of Psychiatry, 139,* 1262-1266.

Dobash, R. E., & Dobash, R. (1979). *Violence against wives.* New York: Free Press.

Drummond, D. J., Sparr, L. F., & Gordon, G. H. (1989). Hospital violence reduction among high-risk patients. *Journal of the American Medical Association, 261*(17), 2531-2534.

Fishbein, D. H., Lozovosky, D., & Jaffe, J. H. (1989). Impulsivity, aggression, and neuroendocrine responses to serotonergic stimulation in substance abusers. *Biological Psychiatry, 25,* 1049-1066.

Frieze, I. H., & Schafer, P. C. (1984). Alcohol use and marital violence: Female and male differences in reactions to alcohol. In S. C. Wilsnack & L. J. Beckman (Eds.), *Alcohol problems in women: Antecedents, consequences, and intervention* (pp. 260-279). New York: Guilford.

George, W. H., Dermen, K. H., & Nochajski, T. H. (1989). Expectancy set, self-reported expectancies and predispositional traits: Predicting interest in violence and erotica. *Journal of Studies on Alcohol, 50*(6), 541-551.

Gondolf, E. W., Mulvey, E. P., & Lidz, C. W. (1990). Characteristics of perpetrators of family and nonfamily assaults. *Hospital and Community Psychiatry, 41*(2), 191-193.

Goodman, R. A., Mercy, J. A., & Loya, F. (1986). Alcohol use and interpersonal violence: Alcohol detected in homicide victims. *American Journal of Public Health, 76*, 144-146.

Goodman, R. A., Mercy, J. A., & Rosenberg, M. L. (1986). Drug use and interpersonal violence. *American Journal of Epidemiology, 124*(5), 851-855.

Gottfredson, D. M., & Gottfredson, S. D. (1988). Stakes and risks in the prediction of violent criminal behavior. *Violence and Victims, 3*(4), 247-262.

Gross, B. H., Southard, M. J., Lamb, R., & Weinberger, L. E. (1987). Assessing dangerousness and responding appropriately: *Hedlund* expands the clinician's liability established by *Tarasoff. Journal of Clinical Psychiatry, 48*(1), 9-12.

Harbison, J. (1991). Clinical decision making in nursing. *Journal of Advanced Nursing, 16*, 404-407.

Holcomb, W. R., & Ahr, P. R. (1988). Arrest rates among young adult psychiatric patients treated in inpatient and outpatient settings. *Hospital and Community Psychiatry, 39*, 52-57.

Jaffe, J. H. (1985). Drug addiction and drug abuse. In A. G. Gilman, L. S. Goodman, T. W. Rall, & F. Murad (Eds.), *The pharmacological basis of therapeutics* (pp. 532-581). New York: Macmillan.

Janofsky, J. S., Spears, S., & Neubauer, D. N. (1988). Psychiatrists' accuracy in predicting violent behavior on an inpatient unit. *Hospital and Community Psychiatry, 39*, 1090-1094.

Josephson, W. L. (1987). Television violence and children's aggression: Testing the priming, social script, and disinhibition predictions. *Journal of Personality and Social Psychology, 53*(5), 882-890.

Krakowski, M., Jaeger, J., & Volavka, J. (1988). Violence and psychopathology: A longitudinal study. *Comprehensive Psychiatry, 29*, 174-181.

Lambert, E. W., Cartor, R., & Walker, G. L. (1988). Reliability of behavioral versus medical models: Rare events and danger. *Issues in Mental Health Nursing, 9*, 31-44.

Lenke, L. (1982). Alcohol and crimes of violence: A causal analysis. *Contemporary Drug Problems, 11*, 355-365.

Lester, D. (1987). Social integration, economic hardship, and rates of personal violence (suicide and homicide): 1933-1970 in the USA. *Psychological Reports, 60*, 1306.

Lewis, D. O., Lovely, R., Yeager, C., & Femina, D. D. (1989). Toward a theory of the genesis of violence: A follow-up study of delinquents. *Journal of the American Academy of Child and Adolescent Psychiatry, 28*(3), 431-436.

Lindquist, P., & Allebeck, P. (1989). Schizophrenia and assaultive behaviour: The role of alcohol and drug abuse. *Acta Psychiatrica Scandanavia, 82*, 191-195.

McNeil, D. E., Binder, R. L., & Greenfield, T. K. (1988). Predictors of violence in civilly committed acute psychiatric patients. *American Journal of Psychiatry, 145*(8), 965-970.

Meloy, J. R. (1987). The prediction of violence in outpatient psychotherapy. *American Journal of Psychotherapy, 61*(1), 38-45.

Menzies, R. J., Webster, C. D., & Sepejak, D. S. (1985). Hitting the forensic sound barrier: Predictions of dangerousness in a pretrial psychiatric clinic. In C. D. Webster, M. H. Ben-Aron, & S. J. Hucker (Eds.), *Dangerousness: Probability and prediction, psychiatry and public policy* (pp. 115-144). New York: Cambridge University Press.

Miller, M., & Morris, N. (1988). Predictions of dangerousness: An argument for limited use. *Violence and Victims, 3*(4), 263-283.

Monahan, J. (1981). *The clinical prediction of violent behavior.* Beverly Hills, CA: Sage.

Monahan, J. (1984). The prediction of violent behavior: Toward a second generation of theory and policy. *American Journal of Psychiatry, 141,* 10-15.

Mulvey, E. P., & Reppucci, N. D. (1988). The context of clinical judgment: The effect of resource availability on judgments of amenability to treatment in juvenile offenders. *American Journal of Community Psychology, 16*(4), 525-545.

Myers, K. M., & Dunner, D. L. (1984). Self- and other-directed violence on a closed acute-care ward. *Psychiatric Quarterly, 56,* 178-188.

Norton, R. N., & Morgan, M. Y. (1989a). Improving information on the role of alcohol in interpersonal violence in Great Britain. *Alcohol and Alcoholism, 24*(6), 577-589.

Norton, R. N., & Morgan, M. Y. (1989b). Mortality from interpersonal violence in Great Britain. *Injury, 20,* 131-133.

Norton, R. N., & Morgan, M. Y. (1989c). The role of alcohol in mortality and morbidity from interpersonal violence. *Alcohol and Alcoholism, 24*(6), 565-576.

Regan-Kubinski, M. J. (1991). A model of clinical judgment processes in psychiatric nursing. *Archives of Psychiatric Nursing, 5*(5), 262-270.

Roberts, A. (1988). Substance abuse among men who batter their mates: The dangerous mix. *Journal of Substance Abuse Treatment, 5,* 83-87.

Robins, L., & Regier, D. (Eds.). (1991). *Psychiatric disorders in America: The epidemiological catchment area study.* New York: Free Press.

Schon, D. (1983a). *The reflective practitioner.* New York: Basic Books.

Schon, D. (1983b). From technical rationality to reflection in action. In J. Dowie & A. Elstein (Eds.), *Professional judgment: A reader in clinical decision making* (pp. 60-77). Cambridge, UK: Cambridge University Press.

Segal, S. P., Watson, M. A., Goldfinger, S. M., & Averbuck, D. S. (1988). Civil commitment in the psychiatric emergency room: The assessment of dangerousness by emergency room clinicians. *Archives of General Psychiatry, 45,* 748-752.

Steadman, H. J. (1986). Predicting violence leading to homicide. *Bulletin of the New York Academy of Medicine, 62*(5), 570-578.

Steadman, H. J., & Morrissey, J. P. (1982). Predicting violent behavior: A note on a cross-validation study. *Social Forces, 61,* 475-483.

Swanson, J., & Holzer, C. (1991). Violence and the ECA data. *Hospital and Community Psychiatry, 42,* 79-80.

Swanson, J. W., Holzer, C. E., Ganju, V. K., & Jono, R. T. (1990). Violence and psychiatric disorder in the community: Evidence from the epidemiologic catchment area surveys. *Hospital and Community Psychiatry, 41*(7), 761-770.

Tarasoff v. Regents of the University of California. 118 Cal Rptr, 129, 529 P.2d 553 (1974).

Tarasoff v. Regents of the University of California. 17 Cal 3d 425, 551 P.2d 334 (1976).

Tardiff, K., & Sweillman, A. (1982). Assaultive behavior among chronic inpatients. *American Journal of Psychiatry, 139,* 212-215.

Werner, P. D., Rose, T. L., & Yesavage, J. A. (1990). Aspects of consensus in clinical predictions of imminent violence. *Journal of Clinical Psychology, 46*(4), 534-538.

2

Prediction Issues for Practitioners

Joel S. Milner
Jacquelyn C. Campbell

❏ Prediction Issues for Practitioners

Practitioners often are called on to predict the dangerousness of clients. Because the situations in which predictions are made vary greatly, some authors have suggested that distinctions be made between formal and informal predictions (e.g., Werner, Rose, & Yesavage, 1990). *Formal prediction* refers to views expressed by professionals in hearings and court proceedings that influence sentencing, parole, and custody decisions. *Informal prediction* refers to comments made by practitioners in clinical situations with criminal justice system officials, health care professionals, victim advocates, and potential victims. Regardless of whether the prediction is formal or informal, however, practitioners are obligated to be as accurate as possible and to have considered the ethical dilemmas of (a) confidentiality versus warning and (b) protection of individual rights versus the collective good.

Although many practitioners may be reluctant to make predictions because of problems with prediction accuracy and ethics, they are constantly under pressure to do so by formal systems, other professionals, clients, and clients' families. For example, practitioners are being used with increased frequency as expert witnesses in cases of sexual and spousal abuse. Although practitioners may be able to avoid becoming involved in formal predictions, there are still legal and ethical mandates for practitioners to make informal predictions of dangerousness, such as when they inform potential victims. Thus practitioners involved in work with violent or potentially violent clients have a great need for understanding the nature, process, and research status of prediction.

❏ Clinical Versus Statistical Prediction Strategies

When discussing different types of prediction, it is useful to make a distinction between clinical and statistical prediction. Miller and Morris (1988) describe *clinical prediction* as being based on professional training, professional experience, and observation of a particular client. *Statistical prediction* involves predicting an individual's behavior on the basis of how others have acted in similar situations (actuarial) or on an individual's similarity to members of violent groups. Such prediction is based on statistical models (e.g., additive linear models, clustering models, contingency tables analysis) and includes the use of risk factor instruments (Gottfredson & Gottfredson, 1988; Miller & Morris, 1988).

The consensus of opinion is that statistical prediction is more accurate than clinical prediction, although they may be used in combination. In fact, whenever possible, we strongly recommend using statistical procedures to increase the accuracy of clinical prediction. A summary of the criteria commonly used in the different types of prediction of violent behavior is presented in Table 2.1. As indicated, informal clinical prediction often occurs without the assistance of validated instruments by using the kinds of models outlined in Chapter 1. In formal prediction, however, statistical methods and/or risk instruments that meet certain psychometric standards should be

Table 2.1 Approaches Commonly Used in the Formal and Informal Prediction
of Violent Behavior

	Formal	*Informal*
Clinical	1 & 2	1
Statistical	3	2

1. Clinical judgment through interview and other subjective assessments.
2. Risk factor identification is used. Construct and validity data are
   needed to support the use of a risk factor instrument.
3. Dichotomous/Criterion/Cutoff scores are used. The assessment
   instrument provides a score designated as the criterion or cutoff that is
   used to place an individual into one category or another. Concurrent
   and future predictive validity data and individual classification rates
   are needed.

NOTE: Although this table is a summary of procedures used in the clinical and statistical
prediction of violence, in all cases multiple data sources should be used in making predictions
regarding violence. Further, when formal statistical prediction is possible, a single test score must
never be used to make a prediction.

used. To this end, Monahan (1993) has emphasized the need for
"familiarity with basic concepts in risk assessment (e.g., predictor
and criterion variables, true and false positives and negatives, decision rules, base rates)" (p. 247). In this chapter we concentrate on
issues related to the use of instruments for prediction. Other statistical prediction methods have been discussed elsewhere (see Gottfredson & Gottfredson, 1988, for an overview) and for the most part have
not been developed specifically for family violence prediction.

❏ Legal Issues and Prediction

Although a few courts have rejected or limited the duty to protect
as stated in *Tarasoff v. Regents of the University of California* (1976), most
state courts have accepted the basic tenet of a duty to protect, with
several courts expanding the concept (Appelbaum, 1988; Knapp,
Vandecreek, & Shapiro, 1990; Monahan, 1993; Schopp, 1991; Smith,
1991). It is now commonly held by legal experts that if a therapist
decides that her or his patient is a serious danger to someone else,

the therapist must warn potential victims (Small, 1985). Therapists who have failed to provide such warnings have been held liable for damages to victims. However, conflicting rulings have been made about the duty to warn when the potential victim already knows about the patient's proclivity for violence, and it is unclear to what extent the therapist is responsible for warning others who potentially may be hurt by the patient.

❏ Ethical Issues and Prediction

In addition to the legal duty to warn, professional organizations of psychiatrists and psychologists have ethical standards of practice that state the therapist must warn potential victims. The American Medical Association's *Principles of Medical Ethics* mandates that physicians protect potential victims of patients by taking action such as notifying law enforcement agencies.

Clinicians have ethical responsibilities to persons in physical danger.

Even without organizationally prescribed ethical standards, clinicians have ethical responsibilities to persons in physical danger. When the probable perpetrator is the client, the legal and ethical mandate to warn and protect potential victims often is in conflict with the mandate of confidentiality. Prediction also involves the possibility (a) that one's own biases will influence one's judgment and (b) of subjecting a person to unfair criminal justice penalties on the basis of an inaccurate prediction. As a result of these dilemmas, clinicians often desire fail-safe prediction instruments so that no judgment is necessary. The reality, of course, is that statistical methods are in various stages of development and that their ability to correctly screen violent and nonviolent individuals will never be totally accurate. Thus the practitioner's knowledge of clinical assessment remains an extremely important adjunct to any statistical prediction. Instrumentation can be a valuable source of objective data, provided that prior use and testing of a measure has supported its reliability and validity. The legal and ethical responsibility of clinicians includes becoming as knowledgeable as possible about the dynamics of violence, particularly in terms of potential for further dangerousness. In addition, there is the need to know about instruments that measure dangerousness in specific areas (e.g., child abuse and spousal abuse, as opposed to general aggressiveness or pathology) and the limits of their use, topics covered in Chapters 3 through 6. In the remainder of this chapter we discuss how one evaluates the psychometric properties of risk assessment instruments.

❏   Psychometric Issues in Clinical Practice

The belief that professionals dealing with violent clients need to increase their knowledge of measurement issues is supported by research findings. For example, Milner (1989) surveyed 550 administrators, researchers, and practitioners in the family violence field to determine their knowledge of appropriate uses of the Child Abuse Potential (CAP) Inventory, a screening scale for physical child abuse (Milner, 1986). The survey revealed that a substantial number of professionals suggested applications for the CAP Inventory that were inappropriate or not supported by validity data. Milner concluded that an increase in professional knowledge of the proper use of child abuse screening instruments should accompany the development of such instruments or the use of family violence screening instruments should be restricted to those who have credentials (e.g., licensed psychologists) to help ensure an adequate knowledge of measurement issues.

In an attempt to increase the practitioner's knowledge of psychometric issues, we discuss some of the traditional psychometric requirements for tests and measures. The reader should note that a comprehensive set of standards has been developed to guide the practitioner in the evaluation and use of test instruments. Psychometric and practice standards are provided in the publication *Standards for Educational and Psychological Testing* (American Psychological Association, 1985). This document includes sections that describe the responsibilities of the test constructor, the test publisher, and the test user.

As standards have evolved, the trend has been toward increasing the responsibility of the test user for the determination that a test is appropriate for a given application. Further, when the test constructor or test publisher does not provide data that support a specific test application (e.g., violence prediction) and the test user nevertheless makes the application, the test user is responsible for providing research evidence to support the new application. Documentation also is needed when the test application is not new but the population under investigation has not been previously studied. In this case, prior to test use, the test user is responsible for collecting data to indicate that the test is still appropriate when used with the new subject population.

❏ Approaches to Developing Predictive Instruments

Ideally the development of an instrument or test is based on a well-defined, empirically validated model that describes etiologic variables. Constructs from the model are used to define the content domains, or areas to be covered by the proposed instrument. Guided by the content domains, a large pool of items is developed and administered to criterion and matched comparison groups. The criterion group is chosen to exemplify or "have" the characteristic being measured. Then an item analysis is conducted to determine the best predictors. After item cross-validation, which involves replicating the predictive ability of the items by using another sample of criterion and comparison subjects, factor analysis can be conducted to provide descriptive factors. Then it is determined whether the total score or some configuration of factor scores most effectively discriminates the criterion subjects from the comparison subjects.

In cases in which explanatory theories are lacking, a combination of rational and empirical approaches can be used to develop test items (Edwards, 1970). In this approach, different theoretical perspectives and empirical studies are used to develop an array of content domains to guide test construction. This technique often is called a "shotgun" approach to test development, wherein all possibly relevant domains are used to guide item development. When there are no well-developed models, however, this technique provides a method for test construction that can result in the successful development of an instrument. A drawback of developing a measure without a guiding explanatory model is that important etiologic variables may be omitted from the content domains used to develop the assessment items.

Fortunately, for a screening instrument to be successful, not all content domains have to be used in the development of the test. Indeed, from a psychometric perspective, the predictive factors need not be related directly to the etiology. A subset of the descriptive factors, whether causal or marker variables, often can be found that are reliably correlated with the criterion behavior (e.g., physical abuse) and that can predict the behavior. Although this approach frequently is criticized, in reality most measures are constructed by using only a subset of the content domains related to the predicted behavior.

❏ Test Reliability

Although many types of reliability are mentioned in the psychometric literature, instrument reliability is of two major types: internal consistency and temporal stability. Internal consistency and temporal stability reliabilities are both statistically represented by correlation coefficients.

INTERNAL CONSISTENCY

Estimates of *internal consistency*, or item consistency, provide information on the equivalence, or homogeneity, of the test items. This equivalence provides an estimate of the degree to which the test items are all measuring the same construct. Internal consistency estimates usually are presented as alpha coefficients. High internal consistency indicates that a test is measuring a specific construct, such as depression. Low internal consistency suggests that more than one construct or a multidimensional construct, such as self-concept, is being assessed.

Internal consistency estimates are affected by test length. A scale with few test items (e.g., 5) must be very homogeneous to have high (e.g., .90) internal consistency, whereas a scale with a large number of test items (e.g., 100) actually may include a variety of different but related items (e.g., distress, anxiety, impulsiveness) and still have a relatively high internal consistency. Test reliability is important because it sets the upper limits for test validity; that is, on average, test validity of an instrument cannot be higher than the internal consistency of the test. In most cases test validity estimates will be lower, sometimes markedly lower, than the internal consistency estimates.

TEMPORAL STABILITY

The *temporal stability* of a test score indicates the degree of test score stability, or how similar test scores are over a specified time period. High levels of temporal stability suggest that the construct being measured tends to be stable over time and that the test is measuring the same construct in the same way across time. Temporal stability estimates are calculated by correlating test scores obtained from the same subject at two points in time. Thus temporal stability estimates are represented by test-retest correlations for different time intervals, such as 1-week, 1-month, 6-month, and 1-year test-retest intervals.

The expected degree of temporal stability of a test score should be high if the test purports to measure a personality trait because these personality characteristics are expected to be stable across time. In contrast the level of acceptable temporal stability of a test score may be relatively modest or low if the test is designed to measure a personality state that is expected to change across time. So the level of test-retest reliability, or temporal stability, should vary as a function of the conceptualization of the construct (trait or state) under investigation.

When evaluating the temporal stability of a test, the extent of gain scores is important to note. *Gain scores* describe test score increases that occur at the second testing, relative to the first testing. Most psychological tests tend to have slightly higher scores at the second testing. Thus, when test-retest reliabilities are presented, the test score means and standard deviations obtained at each test period should be published so that the practitioner can evaluate the size of any gain score.

Test-retest reliabilities and gain scores are of particular concern in certain test applications. For example, in research designs in which multiple evaluations are made at different time intervals, knowledge of the test's temporal stability is critical. Examples of such studies include pre- and posttreatment evaluation research and longitudinal victim effects studies, in which the same measures are administered repeatedly, usually at fixed time intervals. In these designs, only tests with appropriate temporal stability and modest gain scores for the time periods should be used.

❏ **Test Validity**

Validity data provide information on the extent to which a test is adequate for the intended use. In the validation process the inferences made from test scores, not the actual test scores, are validated. As part of the investigation of the psychometric qualities of a test, different types of validity data should be accumulated. It is the accumulated validity evidence from many studies conducted by different investigators, not the evidence from any single study, that allows the user to determine whether the instrument measures what it purports to measure.

Ideally, specific validity data for a particular type of application are accumulated so that the mass of evidence supports or does not support a given test application. Frequently test validity data may indicate that a test is appropriate for one use with a given population, while data may not be available for the same application with another population or for another application with the same population. For example, a prediction instrument may have data from several sources that support predicting future sexual child abuse in white, male perpetrator samples but have little or no data supporting the use of the instrument to predict recidivism in African American perpetrators.

Further, no test should ever be said to be "valid" for its intended use. Test validation is a matter of degree of validity for certain applications with specific populations. Validation is an ongoing process and never a completed task. Test reviews or advertisements that indicate a test is "valid" or has been "fully validated" are inappropriate and misleading. More appropriate is the review or advertisement that indicates substantial data exist demonstrating the test has some degree of validity for a specific application with a specific population or populations. Further, the supporting psychometric data for a test should be available to the test user and other interested professionals in the published literature and in a technical manual. If the relevant validity information is not readily available, the author of the instrument should be contacted to determine whether such information exists.

> *Test validation is a matter of degree of validity for certain applications with specific populations.*

Although different types of test validity have been described, three broad categories of test validity, which contain some overlap, usually are discussed: content, construct, and predictive (post hoc, concurrent, future type) validity. Each of these categories is discussed in the following sections.

CONTENT VALIDITY

The *content validity* of a test refers to the extent to which the test items represent a specific content domain. As previously discussed, the *content domain* typically is defined by the theoretical model on which the test is based. In cases in which no model is used to guide the development of test items, some rational or empirical approach is used to guide the item development, and this approach serves to define the content domains. In either case, the approach used defines the domain or domains that must be sampled adequately during test construction.

The extent to which the test items represent the guiding conceptual domains indicates the degree of content validity. Thus the procedures that guided the construction of the test items and the face validity of the items are used to inform the user about the degree of content validity. Content validity can be demonstrated also by obtaining evaluations of items from experts in the field. In addition, Nunnally (1978) indicates that content validity can be supported by the determination of several types of circumstantial evidence. For example, content validity is supported if the test has moderately high levels of internal consistency. In addition, content validity is supported by construct validity if the test scores are correlated with other measures of constructs representing the content domains used to develop the test items.

CONSTRUCT VALIDITY

Test *construct validity* refers to the extent to which the underlying constructs assumed to be measured by the test actually are measured. Construct data provide verification of what initially was theoretically or intuitively assumed during the test item construction. Construct validity is supported by the accumulation of data that verify that the characteristics the instrument was designed to measure are indeed measured. In addition, development of a large array of different types of construct validity data provides a mosaic of information that allows the test user to understand what the instrument is measuring. Such information serves to assist the user in making more appropriate test score interpretations.

In general, two broad types of construct validity exist: convergent validity and discriminant validity. *Convergent validity* data are generated when factors thought to be related to the test scores are shown to be related. *Discriminant validity* data are generated when factors believed to be extraneous to the test scores are found to be unrelated. Convergent and discriminant validity can be demonstrated by a variety of techniques, such as comparison of test scores with other test scores, with relationships demonstrated only where relationships are expected; demonstration of expected relationships between test scores and different criterion and comparison groups; conceptually congruent factor analysis; and test data from program evaluations that show the test scores are sensitive to treatment effects.

PREDICTIVE VALIDITY

Test predictive validity, or criterion validity, consists of three types: post hoc, concurrent, and future type (Nunnally, 1978). *Post hoc prediction* refers to the prediction of a condition in the past. *Concurrent prediction* refers to the prediction of a condition that presently exists.

Future prediction refers to the prediction of a condition or event that has not yet occurred, which includes both a first occurrence and recidivism. Future prediction, therefore, involves "forecasting" the occurrence of future events on the basis of present test scores. Each of these three types of prediction is needed in the detection and prevention of violence.

Post hoc prediction is very difficult, and this type of validity data is rarely available for a test. The major problem in post hoc prediction is that the test data are collected after the occurrence of the behavior. Although a temporal separation between testing and the predicted behavior also exists for future prediction, as is discussed later, more problems exist for post hoc prediction. Not only can random intervening variables affect test scores and reduce the predictive relationship, but when violence does occur, consequences often result from the occurrence of the behavior. In some cases legal intervention will occur or treatment will be provided. In the case of family violence, children may be removed or a wife may leave. These and other direct consequences of the violence can affect the personality and interactional characteristics of the perpetrator. Therefore subsequent testing of the violent perpetrator may not represent the conditions present at the time of the abuse, making post hoc prediction difficult.

Concurrent predictive validity is especially important when a test is used to place an individual in a particular group (e.g., currently abusive). Although concurrent predictive validity data are often available for a test, most of these data are expressed in terms of group differences, as opposed to individual classification rates; that is, test data typically only indicate that a test shows significant group differences between a criterion group (e.g., physical child abusers) and a comparison group (e.g., nonabusers).

Although group differences must exist if a test is capable of individual subject discrimination, the finding that a test shows significant group differences between criterion and comparison groups does not alone mean that the test has acceptable subject classification ability. Further, many studies that compare groups do not match the criterion and comparison groups on demographic variables, a shortcoming that increases the likelihood that group differences will be found but for the wrong reasons. In cases in which criterion and comparison groups are not matched and group differences are found,

Table 2.2 Types of Individual Classification Outcomes

	Actual Risk Status	
Screened Risk	*Client at Risk*	*Client Not at Risk*
Client at risk	A	B
Client not at risk	C	D

A. Correct classification of at-risk status (sensitivity)
B. Misclassification of risk status (false positive classification)
C. Misclassification of nonrisk status (false negative classification)
D. Correct classification of nonrisk status (specificity)

it is not known whether the group differences are due to the criterion variable or to group demographic differences or to both factors. Thus what is needed to demonstrate adequate individual predictive validity is the individual subject classification rates for test scores based on well-defined criterion and matched comparison groups.

A remaining problem is that most individual classification rates are based on a statistical procedure known as *discriminant analysis.* Although discriminant analysis is appropriate for providing initial estimates of individual predictive validity, this procedure provides optimal classification rates for each sample tested because it reweights the item scores in each new analysis. Therefore, as individual classification data accumulate, some of the data must be obtained by using the test instrument standard scoring procedure designed for field use. Some decrease in the individual correct classification rates can be expected when a standard scoring procedure is used across a variety of demographically different populations.

When individual classification rates are available, the test user should note carefully the percentage of false positive classifications (nonabusers labeled as abusive) and false negative classifications (abusers labeled as nonabusive). Related to these estimates are the sensitivity and specificity of the test. *Test sensitivity* is the percentage of correct classifications of abusers; *test specificity* is the percentage of correct classifications of nonabusers. These four outcomes expressed in terms of risk assessment for violence are presented in Table 2.2.

In most cases in which predictive validity is provided, it is the concurrent type. Future predictive validity, often the most desirable type of validity when violence is under study, is rarely provided. In the few cases in which these data are available, the validity data are typically modest or not significant. In fairness to test developers, it should be mentioned that future prediction is very problematic not only because of the difficulties involved in the design of a predictive instrument but also because numerous variables can intervene between the testing session and the predicted event. These intervening variables may increase or decrease the likelihood of the event, thus reducing the test's predictive ability.

❏ Other Measurement Issues

In addition to the determination that adequate reliability and validity data exist to support a desired test application, a number of other measurement issues must be considered when a test is used to assess interpersonal violence. Several of the more important measurement considerations are (a) the possibility of subject response distortion, (b) the availability of appropriate test norms, (c) the size of the standard error of measurement, and (d) the estimated violence base rates.

RESPONSE DISTORTIONS

A major issue related to the use of self-report measures is the possibility that subjects will distort their responses to the test items. Response distortions include faking-good, faking-bad, and random response behavior. *Faking-good behavior* is related to the respondent's attempt to distort responses in a socially desirable manner or to present him- or herself in a favorable light. *Faking-bad behavior* is related to the respondent's attempt to distort responses in a socially undesirable manner and to present him- or herself in an unfavorable light. *Random response behavior* is related to the respondent giving responses that do not represent responses to the item content. Random responding may be due to a variety of factors, such as a deliberate desire to avoid revealing personal data or an inability to understand item content. A more complete discussion of possible causes of the three types of response distortions is available else-where (e.g., Milner, 1990).

Because response distortions can render test data meaningless, professionals need to include in their assessment package some measures of response distortions (e.g., faking-good, faking-bad, ran-dom response indexes from existing tests such as the Child Abuse Potential [CAP] Inventory [Milner, 1986]). This inclusion is especially important in the assessment of violence perpetrators because these respondents often are motivated to distort responses made to pro-fessionals investigating violence.

TEST NORMS

The interpretation of a test score is aided by the availability of test norms. Norm scores (e.g., test score means, standard deviations) should be available for well-defined populations. The test manual should indicate the year in which the norm data were collected and provide detailed descriptions of the methods used to collect the norm data and the demographic characteristics of the norm group.

Norms may represent local or regional populations or a national probability sampling. In addition, norm data should be presented as a function of gender, ethnic background, age, marital status, educational level, socioeconomic level, number of children, and so on. Thus the test user should expect the test manual to provide numerous test norms, and so he or she must inspect carefully the norm data for possible moderator variable effects. For example, on the Family Environment Scale (FES) (Moos & Moos, 1986) the norm scores for the family conflict scale vary by more than 100% on the basis of family size (e.g., two family members, conflict score $M = 2.11$; five family members, conflict score $M = 4.78$). In this case, failure to consider the number of family members could result in a dramatic misunderstanding of the meaning of the FES conflict score. The problem is actually more serious on this and other tests because often several moderating variables must be considered.

Although national norms are not available for most tests, norms representing the population from which the respondent was drawn usually are required in order to give meaning to the obtained test score. The norm test scores provide population-based values that enable the user to interpret the obtained test scores in relation to those obtained from a similar subject group. Finally, the types of norm values needed can vary as a function of the test application. Thus the practitioner must determine which norm data are needed for the proper interpretation of the test score and whether these norms are available, rather than simply use whatever norms are presented in the test manual.

STANDARD ERROR OF MEASUREMENT

The test user must be aware that all test scores contain measurement error. An estimate of measurement error, the *standard error of measurement* (SEM), should be available for each test scale. The SEM provides an estimate of the variation of the obtained score from the true score. Because the SEM is a standard deviation, it can be used to set a confidence interval around the obtained score so that the range of scores that includes the true score can be known. The SEM is especially important in the prediction of interpersonal violence when test cutoff scores are used to classify the examinee and the examinee's obtained test score is near the test cutoff score. The examinee's obtained test score should be sufficiently beyond the test cutoff score, as determined by the SEM, so that the interpretation that the test score is elevated is less likely to be the result of chance.

VIOLENCE BASE RATES

Professionals need to be aware of the role of base rates in the prediction of behavior. In the prediction of child abuse or any other violent behavior, the base rate affects the amount of incremental prediction added by a measure in the detection of the behavior under investigation. Optimal increases in prediction occur when the base rates are 50%, which means that 50% of the sample or population are the criterion cases (perpetrators of violence). For example, if a test has an 80% correct classification rate for both abusive and nonabusive parents and the test is used in a

> *Professionals need to be aware of the role of base rates in the prediction of behavior.*

situation in which 50% of the subjects tested are abusive (base rate of 50%), then the classification rate is 80% for each group. If the test is administered to 100 subjects, then 40 abusers (80% of 50 abusers) and 40 nonabusers (80% of nonabusers) will be classified correctly, resulting in an 80% overall classification rate and an equal number of false positive and false negative classifications.

When the base rates are lower than 50%, the usefulness of the test in the selection of who is abusive decreases to the point where the test may be inappropriate. For example, if the same test with an 80% correct classification rate is used in a situation in which only 5% of the subjects tested are abusive (base rate of 5%) in a group of 100 subjects, then the ratio of false positive and false negative classifications will vary dramatically. In light of the 80% correct classification rate for abusers, 4 of the 5 abusers will be classified correctly; however, only 80% of the 95 nonabusers will be classified correctly, resulting in 19 false positive classifications. Thus, overall, 23 subjects (4 correct abuser classifications and 19 false positive classifications) will be indicated as abusive, with only 4 of the 23 actually being abusive. This result means that only 17.4% of those classified as abusers are actually abusive, with 82.6% of those labeled abusive being false positive classifications.

It is also true, however, that the number of correct classifications in the 77 subjects classified as nonabusers will increase. In this example only 1 of the 77 subjects classified as nonabusers will be a false positive classification, resulting in a 98.7% correct classification rate for those labeled nonabusers. Thus, as the base rate decreases, the percentage of false positive and false negative classifications will change dramatically from the classification rates derived from studies in which 50% of the subjects are abusive and nonabusive. It is always important, therefore, for the professional to estimate the base rate for the population under study and to determine the relative utility of the test for the intended application.

❏ Summary

As increasing numbers of measures are developed for use in assessing violence potential, professionals will be required to discriminate between those tests that have some utility and those that should be avoided. As previously noted, the responsibility for making adequate test selection and application is increasingly the responsibility of the test user. This responsibility requires that practitioners increase and maintain their knowledge of psychometric issues related to test selection and use.

Clinicians can avoid making formal prediction in the courtroom, but clients who are perpetrators and victims of child, spouse, and sexual abuse are almost impossible to avoid, given the violent nature of our society. Thus clinicians must be able to make reasonably accurate assessments of the potential for future dangerousness in order to fulfill their ethical and legal mandates to warn and protect potential victims. Clinical expertise (appropriate academic, clinical, and legal training, knowledge of the risk literature), coupled with some form of statistical prediction, allows the greatest accuracy of prediction at the present time.

❏ Evaluating an Instrument

As an example of evaluating the utility of an instrument for prediction, we examine the psychometric properties of the Index of Spouse Abuse (ISA) (Hudson & McIntosh, 1981). Although not specifically designed as a prediction instrument, the ISA might be considered a potentially useful instrument for predicting the seriousness of wife abuse. The ISA is a self-report scale designed to be completed by the female victim of spousal abuse. It assesses verbal, emotional, sexual, and physical aggression and was designed to evaluate treatment progress in identified spousal abuse victims. The ISA provides two subscale scores: a severity of physical abuse score (ISA-P) and a severity of nonphysical abuse score (ISA-NP).

Hudson and McIntosh (1981) reported internal consistency reliability estimates (alphas) of .90 and .91 for the ISA-P subscale and .94 to .97 for the ISA-NP subscale. Using African American, Latino, and white pregnant women, McFarlane, Parker, Soeken, and Bullock (1992) reported internal consistency estimates of .87 for the ISA-P subscale and .93 for ISA-NP subscale. Similarly Campbell, Campbell,

Parker, King, and Ryan (in press) found adequate internal consistency reliabilities for an African American sample. These data support the view that each of the ISA subscales is unidimensional. No information is available on the temporal stability (test-retest reliability) of the ISA scales.

The construct validity of the ISA subscales is supported by a factor analysis that yielded the two expected factors (Hudson & McIntosh, 1981). Hudson and McIntosh also reported a number of correlations that indicate the ISA subscales are not associated with factors thought to have relatively little relationship with spousal abuse (discriminant validity) and are associated with factors thought to be related to spousal abuse (convergent validity), albeit some of the expected correlations were modest. In another study Campbell (see Chapter 5, this volume) reported a correlation of .767 between the ISA-P and the Danger Assessment Scale (DA). The DA was designed to assess the risk of homicide in battering relationships. This finding provides support for the view that higher ISA-P scores are associated with more serious wife abuse. The DA is a recently developed instrument, however, and it is unclear to what extent elevated scores on the DA are associated with homicide, which is a low base rate event and therefore is very difficult to predict.

Hudson and McIntosh (1981) reported on the classification ability of the ISA. They reported classification errors for both of the ISA subscales to be 9.3% for a group of abused and nonabused subjects. These rates were found when optimal cutting scores were determined after examination of the cumulative frequency distributions for the scores obtained from the abused and nonabused subjects. Although these results are encouraging, they need to be cross-validated. It is not known to what extent the same cutting scores would discriminate in a different sample. Further, in the description of the nonabused subjects it was not clear how it was determined that the nonabused women were "free from any clinically significant partner or spouse abuse" (Hudson & McIntosh, 1981, p. 876). In another study, McFarlane et al. (1992) also found that the ISA could discriminate abused from nonabused pregnant women, where abuse was identified by a short structured interview. However, in this study there is the possibility of tautological effects resulting from asking the same or similar questions twice.

Little additional information is available on the ISA because it has not been widely used in published studies of wife abuse. Further, a new version of the scale has been published. The new scale, which has been renamed the Partner Abuse Scales, also contains two subscales (marketed as two separate instruments) for physical and nonphysical abuse. Although the authors indicate that the new scales have high reliability and good content and factor validity, along with other supportive construct validity, not all of the research supporting these claims has been published (Hudson, 1990).

In summary, the original ISA scales appear to have adequate internal consistency. However, no data are available on the temporal stability (test-retest reliability) of the ISA scales. This is an important omission. If test items represent constructs that are not stable across time, this variation will make the prediction of future events difficult, if not impossible. Although the ISA was not designed with future prediction in mind, it is still important to know the temporal stability of the ISA across different time intervals because the ISA scale was designed for use in treatment evaluation. If the ISA scores are highly variable across time, it will be difficult to show that score changes across the treatment period are due to treatment effects, and not to test instability. Noteworthy is the fact that initial discriminant validity data are available for concurrent prediction of abuse and non-abuse group membership. Further, cut scores have been established for classification purposes. However, the cut scores need to be cross-validated on additional samples. Finally, additional criterion data (especially behavioral data) are needed to support the view that higher scores on the ISA scales are predictive of more severe levels of spousal abuse. This support requires some evidence that the ISA scales have interval scale characteristics.

❏ References

American Psychological Association. (1985). *Standards for educational and psychological testing.* Washington, DC: Author.

Appelbaum, P. (1988). The new preventive detention: Psychiatry's problematic responsibility for the control of violence. *American Journal of Psychiatry, 145,* 779-785.

Campbell, D., Campbell, J., Parker, B., King, C., & Ryan, J. (in press). The reliability and factor structure of the Index of Spouse Abuse with African American women. *Violence and Victims*.

Edwards, A. L. (1970). *The measurement of personality traits by scales and inventories*. New York: Holt, Rinehart & Winston.

Gottfredson, D. M., & Gottfredson, S. D. (1988). Stakes and risks in the prediction of violent criminal behavior. *Violence and Victims, 3*, 247-262.

Hudson, W. W. (1990). *Partner abuse scales*. Tempe, AZ: Walmyr.

Hudson, W. W., & McIntosh, S. R. (1981). The assessment of spouse abuse: Two quantifiable dimensions. *Journal of Marriage and the Family, 43*, 873-885.

Knapp, S., Vandecreek, L., & Shapiro, D. (1990). Statutory remedies to the duty to protect: A reconsideration. *Psychotherapy, 27*, 291-296.

McFarlane, J., Parker, B., Soeken, K., & Bullock, L. (1992). Assessing for abuse during pregnancy: Frequency and extent of injuries and associated entry into prenatal care. *Journal of the American Medical Association, 267*, 3176-3198.

Miller, M., & Morris, N. (1988). Predictions of dangerousness: An argument for limited use. *Violence and Victims, 3*, 263-284.

Milner, J. S. (1986). *The Child Abuse Potential Inventory: Manual* (2nd ed.). Webster, NC: Psytec.

Milner, J. S. (1989). Applications of the Child Abuse Potential Inventory. *Journal of Clinical Psychology, 45*, 450-454.

Milner, J. S. (1990). *An interpretive manual for the Child Abuse Potential Inventory*. Webster, NC: Psytec.

Monahan, J. (1993). Limiting therapist exposure to *Tarasoff* liability: Guidelines for risk containment. *American Psychologist, 48*, 242-250.

Moos, R. H., & Moos, B. S. (1986). *Family Environment Scale Manual* (2nd ed.). Palo Alto, CA: Consulting Psychologists Press.

Nunnally, J. C. (1978). *Psychometric theory*. New York: McGraw-Hill.

Schopp, R. (1991). The psychotherapist's duty to protect the public: The appropriate standard and the foundation in legal theory and empirical research. *Nebraska Law Review, 70*, 327-360.

Small, L. B. (1985). Psychotherapists' duty to warn: Ten years after *Tarasoff*. *Golden Gate University, Law Review, 15*(2), 271-300.

Smith, S. (1991). Mental health malpractice in the 1990s. *Houston Law Review, 28*, 209-283.

Tarasoff v. Regents of the University of California, 551 P.2d 334 (1976), vacating 529 P.2d 553 (1974).

Werner, P. D., Rose, T. L., & Yesavage, J. A. (1990). Aspects of consensus in clinical prediction of imminent violence. *Journal of Clinical Psychology, 46*, 534-538.

3

Physical Child Abuse Assessment: Perpetrator Evaluation

Joel S. Milner

In the United States almost 3 million reports of child maltreatment were made in 1992 (McCurdy & Daro, 1993). When reports are made to state departments of social services, child protective services workers are required to investigate and to render a timely decision regarding the occurrence of child maltreatment. As part of the investigation process, protective services workers usually attempt to substantiate the report and identify the perpetrator. In many investigations, protective services workers must make decisions based on a limited amount of assessment data.

After physical child abuse is confirmed, case workers must estimate the likelihood of future abuse when they decide to leave the child in or remove the child from the home. In situations in which

AUTHOR'S NOTE: Preparation of this chapter was supported, in part, by National Institute of Mental Health Grant MH34252 to Joel S. Milner.

the child is removed, case workers often must determine whether and when the child should be returned. Although more case data are usually available at the time this decision is made, the assessment task is difficult because case workers must predict events (e.g., physical assault) that may occur in the future.

Recidivism assessment is especially problematic because intervening variables (factors that occur after the assessment) can affect future parenting behavior. Thus, after intervention, the assessment data may indicate low risk of reabuse. Later events (e.g., new stressors), however, may increase the risk potential even though the low-risk determination after intervention was a valid estimate at the time of the evaluation. Although not always possible, one method of reducing recidivism prediction errors caused by intervening variables is to conduct additional assessments at future dates.

> *The assessment task is difficult because case workers must predict events that may occur in the future.*

❑   **Clinical Issues in Physical Child Abuse Risk Assessment**

Although the above discussion of parent assessment focused on the needs of protective service providers, it should be noted that the utility and purpose of risk assessment vary as a function of the type of intervention. Traditionally prevention/intervention programs have been divided into three general types: primary, secondary, and tertiary prevention. *Primary prevention* programs usually assume that all parents are at risk for child abuse, so procedures for determining risk status are not necessary. Primary prevention programs, which attempt to prevent child abuse prior to its occurrence, often are directed at beliefs, practices, and conditions in the community and culture that are thought to increase the likelihood that parents may abuse their children. *Secondary prevention* programs assume that some parents are more at risk for child abuse than other parents. Secondary prevention programs, which also attempt to prevent child abuse prior to its occurrence, usually assess the risk level of parents.

Parents thought to be at risk are offered some type of intervention (e.g., parenting education, home visitation). *Tertiary prevention* programs involve intervention after the occurrence of child abuse (e.g., legal intervention, therapy). These interventions attempt to prevent the recurrence of child abuse (recidivism). As in secondary prevention, assessment of risk is usually an important part of tertiary intervention. As previously noted, assessment of risk is a necessary part of screening reported cases. After the confirmation of abuse, assessment of risk is important in the determination of whether a child should be removed or returned to the parent. Risk assessment is also important in the determination of treatment effects and the prediction of posttreatment recidivism.

The risk factors assessed in secondary and tertiary prevention programs are determined by the child abuse models that guide the programs. A useful organizational model developed by Belsky (1980) describes four ecological levels that may be found in etiologic models of child abuse: the ontogenic, microsystem, ecosystem, and macrosystem levels. The *ontogenic level* refers to individual factors in child abuse. At this ecological level, models focus on parent characteristics. The *microsystem level* refers to family factors. At this ecological level, models target such factors as parent-child interactions, marital discord, and the quality of family relations (e.g., adaptability, cohesion). At the *ecosystem* (community) and *macrosystem* (culture) *levels*, models include such factors as social support, employment stress, and cultural values. In an extension of his organizational model, Belsky (1993) described in greater detail the various "contexts of maltreatment," which include the immediate context (the parent-child interaction) and broader contexts (community, cultural, and evolutionary conditions) thought to influence the likelihood of child maltreatment.

In recent years a large number of physical child abuse models have been developed, and most include factors from several ecological levels. For example, Tzeng, Jackson, and Karlson (1991) describe 25 models of physical child abuse that have been generated by nine different paradigms (e.g., sociocultural, family system, and learning paradigms). Recent developments also include the refinement of extant models, such as current attempts to understand social information processing in the physically abusive parent (e.g., Milner, 1993).

As with physical child abuse models, risk assessment procedures may target a single factor at any ecological level or can be multidimensional and assess multiple factors at different ecological levels. The primary focus of this chapter is on risk assessment of physical child abuse at the ontogenic (parent) and microsystem (family) levels. In practice these are the levels that typically receive professional assessment to determine individual risk even though the community and the culture may maintain conditions that contribute to the risk for violence.

At the individual level, risk factors can be grouped into overlapping domains of demographic/social, biological, cognitive/affective, and behavioral characteristics (e.g., see Milner & Chilamkurti, 1991). Examples of demographic and social risk factors are nonbiological parent, single parent, young parent, lower levels of education, a large number of children, social isolation, and a parent's childhood history of maltreatment. Lower socioeconomic status (SES) is viewed by many as a major risk factor. Although most lower SES parents do not physically abuse their children, lower SES status may be important because it tends to be associated with lower levels of parental affection, poor communication, and negative parent-child interactions. Other covariants of lower income include single parent status, lower intelligence, less formal education, lower levels of physical health, and higher levels of personal distress and psychopathology (e.g., Herrenkohl, Herrenkohl, Teodter, & Yanushefski, 1984).

Putative biological risk factors include neuropsychological, psychophysiological, and physical health problems. Although few data indicate that neurological problems are risk factors for physical child abuse, Elliott (1988) suggested that some disorders (e.g., episodic dyscontrol, antisocial personality, attention deficit disorders), which are associated with neuropsychological deficits, are associated with child abuse. Elliott also suggested that specific cognitive deficits, such as problems in verbal processing, reduce parents' ability to cope with family problems and increase the risk for physical child abuse.

It has been proposed that physical child abusers possess a hyperreactive trait (Knutson, 1978) and are hyperresponsive to stimuli (Bauer & Twentyman, 1985). Although the data are not always consistent (e.g., McCanne & Milner, 1991), psychophysiological studies generally support the view that abusers and at-risk parents are more physiologically reactive to child and stressful non-child-related stimuli. Although the way physiological reactivity contributes to physical child abuse has yet to be demonstrated, autonomic reactivity is thought to increase the likelihood that parents will react to children's behavior with verbal and physical aggression.

Several authors have found that physical child abusers report more physical disabilities and health problems (e.g., Conger, Burgess, & Barrett, 1979; Lahey, Conger, Atkeson, & Treiber, 1984; Milner, 1986b), while others (Steele & Pollock, 1974) have reported that abusers have more psychosomatic illness. Although it is unclear whether abusive parents have more physical health problems or they simply report more physical problems, it does appear that parental reports of frequent physical health problems are associated with an increased risk for parenting problems.

Abusers tend to view their children as being more problematic and intentionally disruptive and disobedient.

Cognitive and affective risk factors represent a broad array of personality characteristics. These factors include poor ego-strength and low self-esteem, and external locus of control, which includes blaming others for one's problems. Child-related cognitive risk factors include inadequate child development knowledge, inappropriate expectations of children's behavior, negative perceptions and evaluations of children's behavior, and "misattributions" of children's responsibility for behavior, including attributions of hostile intent. Thus abusers, compared with independent observers, tend to view their children as being more problematic and intentionally disruptive and disobedient. A comprehensive review of cognitive factors thought to be related to physical child abuse is available elsewhere (Milner, 1993). In general, affective risk factors include emotions that represent negative affectivity (e.g., distress, depression, loneliness, anxiety, anger). Further, although most physical child abusers are not mentally ill, many types of psychopathology appear to increase the risk of parenting problems.

Behavioral risk factors include the use of alcohol and drugs, although the quality of the studies reporting an association between drug use and child abuse has been questioned (e.g., Leonard & Jacob,

1988). Although abusive parents, compared with nonabusive parents, engage in fewer interactions with their children, when abusers do interact they more frequently engage in negative parenting behaviors. For example, they more often use harsh disciplinary strategies, including verbal and physical assault. In addition, abusive parents use less reasoning and explaining, as well as less praise and fewer rewards. Abusive parents also appear to have attachment problems. Beyond child-related interactional problems, abusers exhibit adult interactional problems, often displaying inadequate interpersonal skills. They also report a general inability to cope with life stress.

Familial risk factors overlap with many of the aforementioned individual risk factors. Demographic characteristics, such as the lack of resources and a large number of family members in an inadequate living environment, are risk factors. As the total number of stressors experienced by the family members increases, so does the risk of child maltreatment. Frequent marital discord, including spousal abuse, is viewed increasingly as a risk factor for physical child abuse. Like marital discord, high levels of family verbal and physical conflict and social isolation, as well as the lack of family cohesion and expressiveness, are viewed as factors that increase risk.

❏ Research Issues in Physical Child Abuse Risk Assessment

A major problem that limits our ability to describe and predict physical child abuse is the way the term *physical child abuse* has been operationalized. Initially child maltreatment was not carefully divided into subtypes. Even today, when physical child abuse is separated from child neglect for research purposes, physical child abuse cases may or may not exclude sexual and/or emotional child abuse. As part of the need to consider the specific types (and combinations) of child maltreatment, the study of different forms of each type, as well as whether the case is situational or chronic, also appears warranted. For example, parents who impulsively spank their children and produce mild bruises may be psychologically different from parents who intentionally burn their children. Because most descriptive and predictive physical child abuse research has been based on poorly defined groups, study results are often difficult to replicate. This difficulty adds to the likelihood of classification errors (false positive and false negative classifications) when attempts are made to use study findings to determine risk potential for a specific type of abuse.

Other problems in physical child abuse research contribute to the likelihood of classification errors. Often matched comparison groups are not used, so it is impossible to determine the extent to which group differences are due to the occurrence of physical child abuse or to group demographic differences (e.g., gender, ethnic background, age, educational level). In addition, cross-validation research using an array of subjects is needed because abuse differences may be found for parents from one population but not for parents from a demographically different population. The question also arises: Is abuse by biological parents different from physical child abuse by other caretakers?

Even if concise definitions of physical child abuse are used, research problems remain because the existence of abuse must be indicated by some criterion, which is often the protective services worker's judgment. Unfortunately there is always the likelihood of attenuation (errors) in this and other physical child abuse criteria. Further, because protective services cases usually are used in research, child abuse cases that are not reported are not studied. Indeed most studies include only volunteer subjects, which further limits the representativeness of the results. In addition, most studies use self-report data, and many do not control for response distortion. Finally, most studies investigate and report group differences but do not report individual prediction rates.

❏ Description and Prediction of Physical Child Abuse

In physical child abuse cases, when the practitioner investigates a reported case, assessment data typically are collected through unstructured and structured interviews with the victim, the suspected perpetrator, other family members, and collaterals. Unfortunately, in clinical practice, interviews can be inefficient and often provide only a limited amount of data (Nunnally, 1978). Ammerman and Hersen (1992) point out that, in the assessment of family violence, interviews tend to be biased and are affected by respondent distortions and recall problems. In an attempt to guide professionals in their interviews of violent families, a number of checklists (e.g., Ayoub & Jacewitz, 1982), risk indicators (e.g., Dalgleish & Drew, 1989), and structured interviews (e.g., Child Abuse and Neglect Interview Schedule [Ammerman, Hersen, & Van Hasselt, 1988], Parent Interview and Assessment Guide [Wolfe, 1988]) have been developed. Structured interviews, relative to unstructured interviews, generally are preferred because they are thought to yield more case information.

A major problem with existing clinical interview criteria is that each criterion lacks selectivity; that is, many parents exhibiting one or more of the at-risk criteria will not be abusive, resulting in an excessive number of false positive classifications. Further, physical child abuse often appears to be the result of the interaction of several contributing factors that occur in the absence of buffering conditions (factors that serve to decrease the likelihood of child maltreatment). Checklists and structured interviews typically do not provide information about which factors or group of factors provides the best prediction of child abuse; and the role of buffering variables is almost never discussed. In fairness to the authors of checklists and structured interviews, buffering variables may be excluded from risk assessment criteria because the role of buffering variables has not been fully explicated in the research literature. For example, family support and peer support appear to be important factors in reducing physical child abuse risk (e.g., Egeland, Jacobvitz, & Sroufe, 1988; Hunter & Kilstrom, 1979; Milner, Robertson, & Rogers, 1990), but the specific buffering effects of different types of family and peer support have not been adequately delineated.

It should be noted that even though checklists and structured interviews are available for assessing different types of family violence, relatively few of these instruments have any published validity data. Even when validity data are available, individual classification data are rarely available. Finally, even if an interview can be shown to have adequate psychometric characteristics, the utility of the interview still can vary as a function of the experience and skill of the interviewer.

In addition to the use of checklists and structured interviews, existing personality measures have been used to assess risk for child abuse. In most assessment situations, it is believed that questionnaires account for a larger portion of the variance than checklists and interview procedures. Nunnally (1978) contends that the questionnaire approach is generally superior to interview techniques because questionnaire data replicate and extend the information obtained through interviews and because questionnaires are usually less time consuming and more economical than interviews.

Nevertheless research on the use of existing personality measures to assess child abuse risk status has yielded mixed results. For example, the Minnesota Multiphasic Personality Inventory (MMPI) (Hathaway & McKinley, 1943), a general measure of psychopathology, has been used to distinguish abusers from nonabusers. Although the MMPI initially was believed to have utility in child abuse screening, the successful replication of MMPI profiles that discriminate between abusers and nonabusers has met with only limited success for physical child abuse (e.g, Gabinet, 1979; Griswold & Billingsley, 1969; Paulson, Afifi, Chaleff, Thomason, & Liu, 1975; Paulson, Afifi, Thomason, & Chaleff, 1974). Projective measures also have been used to distinguish abusers from nonabusers. Only a few studies, however, report data on these attempts (e.g., Rorschach Inkblot Test [Derr, 1978; Lerner, 1975]), and at present it is unclear whether projective tests have any utility in the determination of parental risk for physical child abuse.

As a response to the limitations of existing personality measures, several measures have been designed for the specific purpose of screening for physical child abuse. At present, however, most of these new measures do not have adequate reliability and validity data to support their use. For example, only two of the parent assessment measures (the Michigan Screening Profile of Parenting [MSPP; Helfer, Hoffmeister, & Schneider, 1978] and the Child Abuse Potential [CAP] Inventory [Milner, 1986b]) have published validation and cross-validation data on individual concurrent classification rates, and only one child abuse measure (CAP Inventory) has reported individual future predictive validity data. In situations in which current and future risk status is a concern, individual concurrent and future predictive validity data, along with cross-validation data on different populations, is an absolute necessity. In the following section, I review psychometric data on the CAP Inventory, a questionnaire developed for physical child abuse screening and one of the most commonly used physical child abuse assessment instruments. Independent reviews of the CAP Inventory are available elsewhere (e.g., Hart, 1989; Kaufman & Walker, 1986; Melton, 1989).

THE CHILD ABUSE POTENTIAL (CAP) INVENTORY

The initial development of the CAP Inventory is described in two studies (Milner & Wimberley, 1979, 1980) and in a comprehensive technical manual (Milner, 1986b). An interpretive manual for the CAP Inventory scales is available as a supplement to the technical manual (Milner, 1990). Separate from material in the CAP manuals, articles on the applications and limitations of the CAP Inventory have been published (Melton & Limber, 1989; Milner, 1986a, 1986b, 1989b, 1989c, 1990, 1991a).

The CAP Inventory initially was designed for use in child protective services settings to screen parents reported for physical child abuse. The questionnaire was developed because of the frequent need for additional objective information regarding a physical child abuse report. The development of a screening questionnaire for reported physical child abuse cases was viewed as appropriate because abuse base rates in reported cases of physical child abuse range from 35% to 50% in most protective services settings. A 50% base rate is optimal for a test instrument to produce maximal increases in incremental validity. When base rates of occurrence are low, the utility of using a screening instrument is reduced. If base rates are very low (e.g., 5% or 10%), most single test applications will not provide any meaningful increase in prediction. In such cases some form of multiple stage screening should be used that will raise the base rate at each screening stage.

The CAP Inventory is a 160-item, self-report questionnaire that is answered in a forced-choice, agree-disagree format. The current CAP Inventory (Form VI) contains a 77-item physical child abuse scale that includes six descriptive factor scales: distress, rigidity, unhappiness, problems with child and self, problems with family, and problems from others. To detect response distortions, the CAP Inventory contains three validity scales: a lie scale, a random response scale, and an inconsistency scale. The validity scales are used in paired combinations to form three validity indexes: the faking-good index, the faking-bad index, and the random response index. If a response distortion index is elevated, the abuse scale scores may not be an accurate representation of the respondent's "true" score. The applied manual for the CAP Inventory (Milner, 1990) provides an extensive discussion of how the validity indexes should be interpreted. Although the same 77-item physical child abuse scale has been part of the 160-item CAP Inventory since 1977, the validity scales are relatively new, and all three validity scales are contained only in Form VI of the CAP Inventory. Recently two special scales have been added to the CAP Inventory: the ego-strength scale (Milner, 1988, 1990) and the loneliness scale (Mazzucco, Gordon, & Milner, 1989; Milner, 1990). These special scales were developed from existing scale and filler items and were designed to provide the test user with supplemental clinical information on the examinee.

Concurrent Prediction of Physical Child Abuse. Initial abuse scale classification rates based on discriminant analysis for physical child abusers and matched comparison subjects indicated correct classification rates in the 90% range. In recent studies in which more diverse populations have been used, the individual correct classification rates, again based on discriminant analysis, have been in the mid-80% to the low 90% range (e.g., Caliso & Milner, 1992; Milner, Gold, & Wimberley, 1986; Milner & Robertson, 1989). Similar correct classification rates based on discriminant analysis have been reported for Spanish translations of the abuse scale that have been cross-validated on physical child abusers and matched comparison parents in Spain (de Paul, Arruabarrena, & Milner, 1991) and in Argentina (Bringiotti, 1992).

Because discriminant analysis provides optimal classification rates for the sample under investigation, a recent study investigated abuse scale classification rates determined by the standard scoring procedure (Milner, 1989a). In this study 81.4% of the abusers and 99.0% of the comparison parents were classified correctly, for an overall rate of 90.2%. Typically, in studies in which the abuse scale classification rates have been determined for physical child abusers and matched comparison subjects, more false negative than false positive classifications have been reported. This outcome suggests that it is more likely that the abuse scale will fail to detect abusive parents than to misclassify demographically similar nonabusive parents as abusive.

Further, the abuse scale specificity (ability to correctly classify nonabusive parents) has been investigated in a variety of nonabusive groups with acceptable results. For example, 100% correct classification rates have been reported for low-risk mothers (Lamphear, Stets, Whitaker, & Ross, 1985), nurturing mothers (Milner, 1986b, 1989a), and nurturing foster parents (Couron, 1982). In a major study ($N =$ 1,151) of the effects of medical stressors on the abuse scale specificity, no distortions in specificity were found in mothers with vaginal and C-section delivery, with and without complications (Milner, 1991c). However, modest distortions in abuse scale specificity were found when parents of children with specific types of child injury (e.g., severe burns) and illness (e.g., gastric problems) were tested. Although it is possible that distortions in the abuse scale specificity may have been due to undetected child abuse, these data suggest that the abuse scale specificity may be affected to some degree by a parent having a child with medical problems (Milner, 1991c). Thus, although it appears that the abuse scale can be used with mothers of newborns, additional data are needed to determine whether use of the abuse scale in a medical setting with parents of children who have injuries or illness is appropriate.

In general, when abuse scale classification rates have been determined for maltreatment groups other than recently identified, untreated physical child abusers, the classification rates have been lower. For example, Matthews (1985) investigated CAP abuse scale classification rates for "mildly" abusive parents and comparison parents. To provide a stringent test of the abuse scale classification rates, the mild physical child abuse group excluded moderate and severe physical child abusers. In addition, the comparison parents had children with emotional and behavioral problems. Another sample restriction was that both parent groups already were receiving treatment. Using a cutoff score developed from half of the study sample, Matthews (1985) reported a correct CAP abuse scale classification rate of 72.7%.

Couron (1982) studied a physically abusive and neglectful parent group and a comparison parent group and found that when the abuse scale alone was used to predict group membership, the correct classification rate was 72.6%. A discriminant analysis, however, indicated an overall correct classification rate of 90.3% when the abuse score, a stress measure, and demographic characteristics (e.g., marital status, age of parent) were used to predict group membership.

In another study, Haddock and McQueen (1983) reported abuse scale classification rates for institutional physical child abusers and matched nonabusive institutional employees. A discriminant analysis indicated an overall correct classification rate of 92.9% by using the CAP abuse scale, work satisfaction items, and demographic variables to predict group membership. Although this overall classification rate for institutional abusers is encouraging, the institutional abuser classification rate for the CAP abuse scale alone was not reported.

Collectively these data suggest that the CAP abuse scale may have some validity when used as a screening tool with groups other than suspected physical child abusers who are investigated by social services agencies. However, because the CAP abuse scale was designed for use with parents, additional data are needed to determine the extent to which the CAP abuse scale can be used with nonparent groups (e.g., institutional caretakers).

Future Prediction of Physical Child Abuse. In addition to concurrent validity data, longitudinal predictive validity data are available for the abuse scale. Milner, Gold, Ayoub, and Jacewitz (1984) found a highly significant ($p < .0001$) relationship between elevated abuse scores and later physical child abuse in a group of at-risk parents who were in treatment (Omega squared = .32). A modest relationship ($p < .05$) also was found between abuse scores and later child neglect. In another study, Ayoub and Milner (1985) found that abuse scores of mothers of failure-to-thrive infants receiving services were significantly ($p < .01$) related to later instances of child neglect. Both of the aforementioned studies involved testing parents at the beginning of intervention and, therefore, were not recidivism studies. However, the fact that the parents received intervention and the initial abuse scores were still significantly predictive of later abuse and neglect suggests that the abuse scale may have utility in recidivism prediction. Indeed a recidivism study that assesses individuals after intervention might yield better results because testing prior to treatment precludes the possibility that test scores can change because of the intervention.

Although in all studies the total abuse score has been superior to the individual factor scores in predicting abuse, the predictive validity data indicate that some abuse factors are better at predicting concurrent risk and that others are better at predicting future risk. For example, the level of parent-child-related distress appears to be a strong predictor of concurrent risk, whereas a rigid pattern of expectations of child behavior appears to be a better predictor of future abuse even though both factors significantly predict concurrent and future physical child abuse. This finding may be related to the distress factor's tendency to measure situational conditions that change across time, whereas the rigidity factor appears to measure a traitlike condition that is less likely to change across time. Thus, on the basis of the type of prediction desired, the test user may want to consider the extent to which the different factor scores are elevated.

Construct Validity. A comprehensive, albeit not exhaustive, list of the abuse scale construct validity studies by domain is provided in Table 3.1. The construct validity research indicates that the physical child abuse risk factors discussed previously are related generally to abuse scores in the expected manner. For example, individuals with childhood histories of physical abuse tend to earn higher abuse scores than subjects without such histories. In general, individuals with elevated abuse scores report more family conflict, less family cohesion, and more social isolation. When supportive relationships (adult or peer) occur during childhood, however, the abuse scores reflect these buffering events and tend to be lower. An inverse relationship has been observed between abuse scores and self-esteem and ego-strength. Persons with elevated abuse scores also tend to have an external locus of control. Elevated abuse scores appear to be related to two types of external control orientations: control by chance factors and control by powerful others.

As expected, elevated abuse scores have been associated with higher levels of life stress and personal distress. Further, subjects

Table 3.1 Summary of CAP Inventory Construct Validity Research

---

History of child abuse, receipt and observation
   Caliso & Milner, 1992; Chan & Perry, 1981; Crouch, 1993; Mee, 1983;
   Miller, Handal, Gilner, & Cross, 1991; Milner, Robertson, & Rogers,
   1990

Problems in family functioning
   Arruabarrena & de Paul, 1992; Caliso & Milner, 1992; Chan & Perry,
   1981; Kolko, Kazdin, Thomas, & Day, 1993; Lamphear, Stets, Whitaker,
   & Ross, 1985; Mollerstrom, Patchner, & Milner, 1992; Nealer, 1992;
   Poteat, Grossnickle, Cope, & Wynne, 1990; Whissell, Lewko, Carriere,
   & Radford, 1990

Social isolation/lack of social support
   Burge, 1982; Caliso & Milner, 1994; Crouch, 1993; Kirkham, Schinke,
   Schilling, Meltzer, & Norelius, 1986; Matthews, 1985; Talbott (cited in
   Milner, 1986b); Whissell et al., 1990

Low self-esteem and poor ego-strength
   Chan & Perry, 1981; Fulton, Murphy, & Anderson, 1991; Leak &
   Langholdt (cited in Milner, 1986b); Milner, 1988; Robertson & Milner,
   1983, 1985; Robitaille, Jones, Gold, Robertson, & Milner, 1985; Whissell
   et al., 1990

External locus of control
   Ellis & Milner, 1981; Stringer & La Greca, 1985

Life stress
   Burge, 1982; Couron, 1982; Holden, Willis, & Foltz, 1989; Karr, Becker,
   & Smith, 1988; Mee, 1983; Milner, 1991c; Milner, Charlesworth, Gold,
   Gold, & Friesen, 1988; Talbott (cited in Milner, 1986b)

Physiological reactivity to child- and non-child-related stimuli
   Casanova, Domanic, McCanne, & Milner, 1992; Crowe & Zeskind,
   1992; Hager, 1987; Pruitt & Erickson, 1985

Anger associated with child interactions
   Aragona, 1983; Hager, 1987

Knowledge of child development
   Fulton et al., 1991; Osborne, Williams, Rappaport, & Tuma, 1986;
   Whissell et al., 1990

Perceptions of child's behavior
   Aragona, 1983; Kolko et al., 1993; Stringer, 1983

Evaluations of children's behavior
   Chilamkurti & Milner, 1993

Attributions regarding children's behavior
   Milner & Foody, 1993

---

continued

Table 3.1 Continued

Parenting styles
  Aragona, 1983; Chilamkurti & Milner, 1993; Hann, 1989; Kirkham
  et al., 1986; Kolko et al., 1993; Osborne et al., 1986; Schellenbach,
  Monroe, & Merluzzi, 1991; Stringer, 1983

Assertiveness skills
  Mee, 1983

Authoritarianism
  Bardua, 1987; Robitaille et al., 1985; Whissell et al., 1990

Frustration/aggression
  Matthews, 1985; Pruitt, 1983; Robertson & Milner, 1985; Robitaille
  et al., 1985

Depression
  Arruabarrena & de Paul, 1992; Kirkham et al., 1986; Matthews, 1985;
  Milner et al., 1988; Nealer, 1992; Robitaille et al., 1985; Talbott (cited in
  Milner, 1986b)

Anxiety
  Aragona, 1983; Matthews, 1985; Pruitt, 1983; Robertson & Milner, 1985;
  Talbott (cited in Milner, 1986b)

Mental health/pathology
  Kolko et al., 1993; Matthews, 1985; Pruitt, 1983; Robertson & Milner,
  1985

Other maltreatment and high-risk groups
  Atten & Milner, 1987; Ayoub, Jacewitz, Gold, & Milner, 1983; Ayoub &
  Milner, 1985; Barth, 1989; Couron, 1982; Haddock & McQueen, 1983;
  Holden et al., 1989; Milner & Ayoub, 1980; Milner & Robertson, 1989,
  1990; Milner, 1986b; Talbott (cited in Milner, 1986b); Thomasson,
  Berkovitz, Minor, Cassle, McCord, & Milner, 1981

Low-risk groups
  Couron, 1982; Lamphear et al., 1985; Milner, 1986b, 1989a

Evaluation of intervention/treatment programs
  Barth, 1989; D'Agostino, Chapin, & Moore, 1984; Fulton et al., 1991;
  NCPCA, 1992; Talbott (cited in Milner, 1986b); Thomasson et al., 1981;
  Vogel, 1987; Wolfe, Edwards, Manion, & Koverola, 1988

---

with elevated abuse scores tend to be more physiologically reactive
to both child-related and non-child-related stimuli. Those with elevated abuse scores also report more negative perceptions of their
children's behavior and are more critical and less praising of their
children. Parents with elevated abuse scores display a rigid interac-

tional style and are less responsive to temporal changes in their children's behavior. They make more negative interpretations and evaluations of their children's behavior, use more verbal and physical punishment, and react to children in a controlling and rejecting manner. Elevated abuse scores and stress interact, increasing the parent's aversive, child-directed behaviors. Given these findings, it is not surprising that parents with elevated abuse scores report less satisfaction with the quality of their child attachments.

Additional research indicates that individuals with elevated abuse scores tend to be depressed, moody, touchy, emotionally labile, overreactive, and aggressive. Similarly those with elevated abuse scores have been described as lacking emotional stability, having a low frustration tolerance, being irritable, having poor impulse control, having temper outbursts, and being assaultive.

Although individual classification rates are not always adequate, studies of child maltreatment groups other than physical child abusers indicate that the abuse scale distinguishes groups in the expected manner. For example, the abuse scale discriminates between groups of at-risk and comparison subjects and between groups thought to differ in levels of risk. Abuse scores have distinguished between institutional child abusers and a nonabusive comparison (employee) group and among physical child abusers, intrafamilial sexual child abusers, child neglecters, and three matched comparison groups. Because of common perpetrator characteristics, however, the abuse scale did not adequately discriminate between the different child maltreatment groups.

A number of studies have reported abuse score decreases after intervention.

A number of studies have reported abuse score decreases after intervention. For example, pretreatment, posttreatment, and follow-up abuse score decreases have been reported for at-risk parents presented an ecologically based intervention program. Pretreatment and follow-up abuse score decreases have been found for at-risk parents given a behavioral parent training program. Pre- and posttreatment abuse score decreases have been reported also for a group of abusive and neglectful parents after an intensive multimodal intervention program. Several studies have reported abuse score decreases after in-home

treatments. Finally, initial (very high) abuse scores have been reported to be predictors of client dropout. Collectively the treatment
evaluation studies indicate that the CAP abuse scale is a useful global
measure of treatment effects for at-risk and abusive parent treatment
programs.

Reliability. The CAP Inventory abuse scale internal consistency
(KR-20) reliabilities range from .91 to .96 for general population (n =
2,062), at-risk (n = 124), neglectful (n = 209), and physically abusive
(n = 149) groups (Milner, 1986b). Similar abuse scale internal consistency estimates are reported across gender, age, education, and
ethnic subgroups (Milner, 1986b). The physical child abuse scale
temporal stability (test-retest) reliabilities are .91, .90, .83, and .75 for
general population subjects across 1-day, 1-week, 1-month, and 3-
month intervals, respectively (Milner, 1986b). Additional internal
consistency and temporal stability estimates are available for each of
the three validity scales and for each of the six descriptive factor
scales (Milner, 1986b). Although not presented here, the internal
consistency reliabilities for each of the six abuse factor scales are
lower and more variable than the full abuse scale reliabilities (Milner,
1986b).

OTHER MEASURES FREQUENTLY
USED IN PHYSICAL ABUSE ASSESSMENT

A self-report questionnaire initially developed to screen for physical child abuse is the Michigan Screening Profile of Parenting (MSPP)
(Helfer et al., 1978; Schneider, 1982). As a consequence of validity
research, however, the authors have expanded the scope of the MSPP
and now recommend the scale be used for the screening of parents
with problems in parenting, rather than for the screening of physical
child abuse. Although the individual classification rates for physical
child abusers are adequate and are equal to other measures, research
indicates that the MSPP has high rates of false positive classifications
even in nurturing parent groups (e.g., Schneider, 1982).

A well-known self-report survey instrument that includes a brief
physical child abuse subscale is the Conflict Tactics Scale (CTS)
(Straus & Gelles, 1990). In addition to the special physical child abuse

scale, the CTS contains three subscales: the reasoning scale, the verbal aggression scale, and the violence scale. At present, however, no validity data are available on the individual classification rates of the physical child abuse subscale.

Another self-report measure, the Parenting Stress Index (PSI) (Abidin, 1983), has been developed to assess parent and child-related stress separate from general life stress. This scale appears to be a useful measure of parenting stress and has distinguished groups of physical child abusers and comparison parents. Although the test manual contains many validity studies, no data are available on the individual classification rates of the PSI scale in groups of physical child abusers and matched comparison parents. In light of the sound psychometric base of the PSI, additional data on abusers are needed even though the PSI was not initially designed to screen for physical child abuse.

Finally, a self-report measure, the Adult/Adolescent Parenting Inventory (AAPI), has been developed to assess parent and adolescent attitudes and expectations (Bavolek, 1984, 1989) with respect to children. As with many attitude and personality measures, the AAPI has been shown to distinguish between groups of physical child abusers and comparison parents. However, individual classification rates for physical child abusers and comparison parents are not available. Individual classification rates are especially important because, in addition to the AAPI, there are almost 100 measures of parental attitudes toward child rearing (e.g., Holden & Edwards, 1989), and it is not clear which of these scales, if any, might provide adequate individual classification rates for abuse or risk status.

In addition to the aforementioned measures that are used frequently in physical child abuse risk assessment, other individual and family measures have been developed that may have some utility in child abuse assessment. Additional reviews of physical child abuse assessment techniques are provided elsewhere (e.g., Hansen & MacMillan, 1990; Hansen & Warner, 1992; Milner, 1991b). Comprehensive reviews of individual and family measures that provide information on a wide variety of problems that may occur in families are also available (e.g., Grotevant & Carlson, 1989; Touliatos, Perlmutter, & Straus, 1990).

In conclusion, it should be mentioned that because of the widespread interest in risk assessment, the National Center on Child

Abuse and Neglect (NCCAN) currently is supporting the development and testing of a number of risk assessment protocols. A discussion of risk assessment problems and ongoing risk assessment research is provided in the conference proceedings *Symposium on Risk Assessment in Child Protective Services* (Cicchinelli, 1991), sponsored by NCCAN. Although their description is beyond the scope of this chapter, these risk assessment systems include perpetrator factors, as well as factors from each of the other ecological levels previously mentioned in the description of Belsky's (1980) ecological model. It also appears that these systems have different purposes (e.g., current abuse risk vs. recidivism prediction).

McDonald and Marks (1991) have described and evaluated some of the major risk-assessment systems. Their review includes the following assessment systems: the Alameda County California Re-abuse Assessment Model, the Washington Risk Factor Matrix, the Illinois CANTS 17B, the Utah Risk Assessment Model, the Florida Health and Rehabilitation Services Child Risk Assessment Matrix, the Child Welfare League Family Risk Scales, and the Action for Child Protection-Child at Risk Scales. With respect to the content of the scales, McDonald and Marks conclude, "There is little empirical support for most of the included variables," yet indicate that "subsets of variables can be identified that are common to most instruments and that have empirical support" (p. 112). At present the relative usefulness of each of these systems remains to be established. Further, the need remains to compare assessments by using these systems with other forms of assessment (e.g., questionnaires) and to determine the utility of using these systems in combination with other approaches.

❏ **Summary**

An array of adult risk characteristics for physical child abuse have been identified (see Table 3.1) that can be used to guide any risk assessment. However, not all clients will have all of these characteristics. It is also not clear which risk characteristics or combinations of risk characteristics are the best predictors of physical child abuse.

Further, the available risk assessment techniques (e.g., structured interviews, tests) have varying degrees of reliability and validity. Test users must remember that a measure may have adequate validity for one particular application (e.g., program evaluation) with one population (e.g., adult parents) and not be appropriate for another application (e.g., future prediction) with another population (e.g., adolescent mothers). At present it appears that the best overall risk prediction can be obtained when risk assessment includes data on risk factors from as many sources as possible. These sources include structured parent interviews, collateral interviews, direct observations, and testing with multiple objective measures. When risk factors appear across data sources, the emerging factors can be used collectively to make an estimate of overall risk, with an awareness that mistakes in risk assessment still will occur, especially in situations in which abuse rates are low in the population under investigation.

❏ **References**

Abidin, R. R. (1983). *Parenting Stress Index: Manual.* Charlottesville, VA: Pediatric Psychology Press.

Ammerman, R. T., & Hersen, M. (1992). Current issues in the assessment of family violence. In R. T. Ammerman & M. Hersen (Eds.), *Assessment of family violence: A clinical and legal sourcebook* (pp. 3-10). New York: John Wiley.

Ammerman, R. T., Hersen, M., & Van Hasselt, V. B. (1988). *The Child Abuse and Neglect Interview Schedule (CANIS).* Unpublished instrument, Western Pennsylvania School for Blind Children, Pittsburgh.

Aragona, J. A. (1983). Physical child abuse: An interactional analysis (Doctoral dissertation, University of South Florida, 1983). *Dissertation Abstracts International, 44,* 1225B.

Arruabarrena, M. I., & de Paul, J. (1992). Validez convergente de la version española preliminar del Child Abuse Potential Inventory: Depresion y adjuste marital. *Child Abuse & Neglect, 16,* 119-126.

Atten, D. W., & Milner, J. S. (1987). Child abuse potential and work satisfaction in day care employees. *Child Abuse & Neglect, 11,* 117-123.

Ayoub, C., & Jacewitz, M. M. (1982). Families at risk of poor parenting: A model for service delivery, assessment, and intervention. *Child Abuse & Neglect, 6,* 351-358.

Ayoub, C., Jacewitz, M. M., Gold, R. G., & Milner, J. S. (1983). Assessment of a program's effectiveness in selecting individuals "at risk" for problems in parenting. *Journal of Clinical Psychology, 39,* 334-339.

Ayoub, C., & Milner, J. S. (1985). Failure-to-thrive: Parental indicators, types, and outcomes. *Child Abuse & Neglect, 9,* 491-499.

Bardua, K. (1987). *An exploratory investigation of the characteristics of abusive and neglectful mothers with special reference to rigidity, authoritarianism, and intellectual ability.* Unpublished manuscript.

Barth, R. P. (1989). Evaluation of a task-centered child abuse prevention program. *Children and Youth Services Review, 11,* 117-131.

Bauer, W. D., & Twentyman, C. T. (1985). Abusing, neglectful, and comparison mothers' responses to child-related and non-child-related stressors. *Journal of Consulting and Clinical Psychology, 53,* 335-343.

Bavolek, S. J. (1984). *Adult-Adolescent Parenting Inventory (AAPI).* Eau Clair, WI: Family Development Resources.

Bavolek, S. J. (1989). Assessing and treating high-risk parenting attitudes. In J. T. Pardeck (Ed.), *Child abuse and neglect: Theory, research, and practice* (pp. 97-110). New York: Gordon & Breach.

Belsky, J. (1980). Child maltreatment: An ecological integration. *American Psychologist, 35,* 320-335.

Belsky, J. (1993). Etiology of child maltreatment: A developmental-ecological analysis. *Psychological Bulletin, 114,* 413-434.

Bringiotti, M. I. (1992, September). *Adaptacion y validation del Child Abuse Potential Inventory—CAP: Version preliminar para la Argentina.* Paper presented at the meeting of the International Congress on Child Abuse and Neglect, Chicago, IL.

Burge, E. B. (1982). Child abusive attitudes and life changes in an overseas military environment (Doctoral dissertation, United States International University, 1982). *Dissertation Abstracts International, 43,* 562A.

Caliso, J. A., & Milner, J. S. (1992). Childhood history of abuse and child abuse screening. *Child Abuse & Neglect, 16,* 647-659.

Caliso, J. A., & Milner, J. S. (1994). Childhood physical abuse, childhood social support, and adult child abuse potential. *Journal of Interpersonal Violence, 9,* 27-44.

Casanova, G. M., Domanic, J., McCanne, T. R., & Milner, J. S. (1992). Physiological responses to non-child-related stressors in mothers at risk for child abuse. *Child Abuse & Neglect, 16,* 31-44.

Chan, D. A., & Perry, M. A. (1981, April). *Child abuse: Discriminating factors toward a positive outcome.* Paper presented at the meeting of the Society for Research in Child Development, Boston, MA.

Chilamkurti, C., & Milner, J. S. (1993). Perceptions and evaluations of child transgressions and disciplinary techniques in high- and low-risk mothers and their children. *Child Development, 64,* 1801-1814.

Cicchinelli, L. F. (Ed.). (1991). *Proceedings of a symposium on risk assessment in child protective services.* Washington, DC: National Center on Child Abuse and Neglect.

Conger, R. D., Burgess, R., & Barrett, C. (1979). Child abuse related to life changes and perceptions of illness: Some preliminary findings. *Family Coordinator, 28,* 73-78.

Couron, B. L. (1982). Assessing parental potentials for child abuse in contrast to nurturing (Doctoral dissertation, United States International University, 1981). *Dissertation Abstracts International, 43,* 3412B.

Crouch, J. (1993, July). *Effects of childhood physical abuse and perceived social support on adult socio-emotional functioning.* Paper present at the meeting of the European Congress of Psychology, Tampere, Finland.

Crowe, H. P., & Zeskind, P. S. (1992). Psychophysiological and perceptual responses to infant cries varying in pitch: Comparison of adults with low and high scores on the Child Abuse Potential Inventory. *Child Abuse & Neglect, 16,* 19-29.

D'Agostino, R. A., Chapin, F., & Moore, J. B. (1984). *Rainbow Family Learning Center: Help for parents and haven for children.* Paper presented at the Fifth Congress on Child Abuse and Neglect, Montreal, Canada.

Dalgleish, L. I., & Drew, E. C. (1989). The relationship of child abuse indicators to the assessment of perceived risk and to the court's decision to separate. *Child Abuse & Neglect, 13,* 491-506.

de Paul, J., Arruabarrena, I., & Milner, J. S. (1991). Validacion de una version española del Child Abuse Potential Inventory para su uso en España. *Child Abuse & Neglect, 15,* 495-504.

Derr, J. (1978). Using the Rorschach Inkblot Test in the assessment of parents charged with child abuse and neglect. *British Journal of Projective Psychology and Personality Study, 23,* 29-31.

Egeland, B., Jacobvitz, D., & Sroufe, L. A. (1988). Breaking the cycle of violence. *Child Development, 59,* 1080-1088.

Elliott, F. A. (1988). Neurological factors. In V. B. Van Hasselt, A. S. Morrison, A. S. Bellack, & M. Hersen (Eds.), *Handbook of family violence* (pp. 359-382). New York: Plenum.

Ellis, R., & Milner, J. S. (1981). Child abuse and locus of control. *Psychological Reports, 48,* 507-510.

Fulton, A. M., Murphy, K. R., & Anderson, S. L. (1991). Increasing adolescent mothers' knowledge of child development: An intervention program. *Adolescence, 26,* 73-81.

Gabinet, L. (1979). MMPI profiles of high-risk and outpatient mothers. *Child Abuse & Neglect, 3,* 373-379.

Griswold, B. B., & Billingsley, A. (1969). *Personality and social characteristics of low-income mothers who neglect and abuse their children* (Final report, PR11001R). Washington, DC: Department of Health, Education and Welfare, Children's Bureau.

Grotevant, H. D., & Carlson, C. I. (1989). *Family assessment: A guide to methods and measures.* New York: Guilford.

Haddock, M. D., & McQueen, W. M. (1983). Assessing employee potentials for abuse. *Journal of Clinical Psychology, 39,* 1021-1029.

Hager, J. C. (1987). *Facial muscular action measured visually and with EMG* (Final Report, MH40577). Washington, DC: National Institute of Mental Health.

Hann, D. M. (1989). A systems conceptualization of the quality of mother-infant interaction. *Infant Behavior and Development, 12,* 251-263.

Hansen, D. J., & MacMillan, V. M. (1990). Behavioral assessment of child-abusive and neglectful families: Recent developments and current issues. *Behavior Modification, 14,* 255-278.

Hansen, D. J., & Warner, J. E. (1992). Child physical abuse and neglect. In R. T. Ammerman & M. Hersen (Eds.), *Assessment of family violence: A clinical and legal sourcebook* (pp. 123-147). New York: John Wiley.

Hart, S. N. (1989). Review of the Child Abuse Potential Inventory, Form VI. In J. C. Conoley & J. J. Kramer (Eds.), *The tenth mental measurements yearbook* (pp. 152-153). Lincoln, NE: Buros Institute of Mental Measurements.

Hathaway, S. R., & McKinley, J. C. (1943). *The Minnesota Multiphasic Personality Inventory.* Minneapolis: University of Minnesota Press.

Helfer, R. E., Hoffmeister, J. K., & Schneider, C. J. (1978). *MSPP: A manual for the use of the Michigan Screening Profile of Parenting.* Boulder, CO: Test Analysis and Development Corp.

Herrenkohl, E. C., Herrenkohl, R. C., Toedter, L., & Yanushefski, A. M. (1984). Parent-child interaction in abusive and nonabusive families. *Journal of the American Academy of Child Psychiatry, 23,* 641-648.

Holden, E. W., Willis, D. J., & Foltz, L. (1989). Child abuse potential and parenting stress: Relationships in maltreating parents. *Psychological Assessment: A Journal of Consulting and Clinical Psychology, 1,* 64-67.

Holden, G. W., & Edwards, L. A. (1989). Parental attitudes toward child rearing: Instruments, issues, and implications. *Psychological Bulletin, 106,* 29-58.

Hunter, R., & Kilstrom, N. (1979). Breaking the cycle in abusive families. *American Journal of Psychiatry, 134,* 1320-1322.

Karr, S. K., Becker, A. H., & Smith, K. L. (1988, April). *Relationship between personality hardiness and child abuse potential.* Paper presented at the meeting of the Southwestern Psychological Association, Tulsa, OK.

Kaufman, K. L., & Walker, C. E. (1986). The Child Abuse Potential Inventory. In D. J. Keyser & R. C. Sweetland (Eds.), *Tests critiques* (Vol. 5, pp. 55-64). Kansas City, MO: Test Corporation of America.

Kirkham, M. A., Schinke, S. P., Schilling, R. F., Meltzer, N. J., & Norelius, K. L. (1986). Cognitive-behavioral skills, social supports, and child abuse potential among mothers of handicapped children. *Journal of Family Violence, 1,* 235-245.

Knutson, J. F. (1978). Child abuse as an area of aggression research. *Journal of Pediatric Psychology, 3,* 20-27.

Kolko, D. J., Kazdin, A. E., Thomas, A. M., & Day, B. (1993). Heightened child physical abuse potential: Child, parent, and family dysfunction. *Journal of Interpersonal Violence, 8,* 169-192.

Lahey, B. B., Conger, R. D., Atkeson, B. M., & Treiber, F. A. (1984). Parenting behavior and emotional status of physically abusive mothers. *Journal of Consulting and Clinical Psychology, 52,* 1062-1071.

Lamphear, V. S., Stets, J. P., Whitaker, P., & Ross, A. O. (1985, August). *Maladjustment in at-risk for physical child abuse and behavior problem children: Differences in family environment and marital discord.* Paper presented at the meeting of the American Psychological Association, Los Angeles, CA.

Leonard, K. E., & Jacob, T. (1988). Alcohol, alcoholism, and family violence. In V. B. Van Hasselt, R. L. Morrison, A. S. Bellack, & M. Hersen (Eds.), *Handbook of family violence* (pp. 147-166). New York: Plenum.

Lerner, P. M. (1975). Rorschach measures of family interaction: A review. In P. M. Lerner (Ed.), *Handbook of Rorschach Scales* (pp. 55-67). New York: International University Press.

Matthews, R. D. (1985). Screening and identification of child abusing parents through self-report inventories (Doctoral dissertation, Florida Institute of Technology, 1984). *Dissertation Abstracts International, 46,* 650B.

Mazzucco, M., Gordon, R. A., & Milner, J. S. (1989). *Development of a loneliness scale for the Child Abuse Potential Inventory.* Paper presented at the meeting of the Southeastern Psychological Association, Washington, DC.

McCanne, T., & Milner, J. S. (1991). Psychophysiological reactivity of physically abusive and at-risk subjects to child-related stimuli. In J. Milner (Ed.), *Neuropsychology of aggression* (pp. 147-166). Norwell, MA: Kluwer.

McCurdy, K., & Daro, D. (1993). *Current trends in child abuse reporting and fatalities: The results of the 1992 annual fifty state survey* (Working paper number 808). Chicago: National Center on Child Abuse Prevention Research.

McDonald, T., & Marks, J. (1991). A review of risk factors assessed in child protective services. *Social Service Review, 65,* 112-132.

Mee, J. (1983). *The relationship between stress and the potential for child abuse.* Unpublished master's thesis, Macquarie University, Australia.

Melton, G. B. (1989). Review of the Child Abuse Potential Inventory, Form VI. In J. C. Conoley & J. J. Kramer (Eds.), *The tenth mental measurements yearbook* (pp. 153-155). Lincoln, NE: Buros Institute of Mental Measurements.

Melton, G. B., & Limber, S. (1989). Psychologists' involvement in cases of child maltreatment: Limits of role and expertise. *American Psychologist, 44,* 400-411.

Miller, T. R., Handal, P. J., Gilner, F. H., & Cross, J. F. (1991). The relationship of abuse and witnessing violence on the Child Abuse Potential Inventory with black adolescents. *Journal of Family Violence, 6,* 351-363.

Milner, J. S. (1986a). Assessing child maltreatment: The role of testing. *Journal of Sociology and Social Welfare, 13,* 64-76.

Milner, J. S. (1986b). *The Child Abuse Potential Inventory: Manual* (2nd ed.). Webster, NC: Psytec.

Milner, J. S. (1988). An ego-strength scale for the Child Abuse Potential Inventory. *Journal of Family Violence, 3,* 151-162.

Milner, J. S. (1989a). Additional cross-validation of the Child Abuse Potential Inventory. *Psychological Assessment: A Journal of Consulting and Clinical Psychology, 1,* 219-223.

Milner, J. S. (1989b). Applications and limitations of the Child Abuse Potential Inventory. *Early Child Development and Care, 42,* 85-97.

Milner, J. S. (1989c). Applications of the Child Abuse Potential Inventory. *Journal of Clinical Psychology, 45,* 450-454.

Milner, J. S. (1990). *An interpretive manual for the Child Abuse Potential Inventory.* Webster, NC: Psytec.

Milner, J. S. (1991a). Additional issues in child abuse assessment. *American Psychologist, 46,* 80-81.

Milner, J. S. (1991b). Measuring parental personality characteristics and psychopathology in child maltreatment research. In R. H. Starr & D. Wolfe (Eds.), *The effects of child abuse and neglect: Issues and research* (pp. 164-185). New York: Guilford.

Milner, J. S. (1991c). Medical conditions and Child Abuse Potential Inventory specificity. *Psychological Assessment: A Journal of Consulting and Clinical Psychology, 3,* 208-212.

Milner, J. S. (1993). Social information processing and physical child abuse. *Clinical Psychology Review, 13,* 275-294.

Milner, J. S., & Ayoub, C. (1980). Evaluation of "at risk" parents using the Child Abuse Potential Inventory. *Journal of Clinical Psychology, 36,* 945-948.

Milner, J. S., Charlesworth, J. R., Gold, R. G., Gold, S. R., & Friesen, M. R. (1988). Convergent validity of the Child Abuse Potential Inventory. *Journal of Clinical Psychology, 44,* 281-285.

Milner, J. S., & Chilamkurti, C. (1991). Physical child abuse perpetrator characteristics: A review of the literature. *Journal of Interpersonal Violence, 6,* 345-366.

Milner, J. S., & Foody, R. (1993). *Impact of mitigating information on attributions for children's behavior in high- and low-risk for physical child abuse subjects.* Manuscript submitted for publication.

Milner, J. S., Gold, R. G., Ayoub, C., & Jacewitz, M. M. (1984). Predictive validity of the Child Abuse Potential Inventory. *Journal of Consulting and Clinical Psychology, 52,* 879-884.

Milner, J. S., Gold, R. G., & Wimberley, R. C. (1986). Prediction and explanation of child abuse: Cross-validation of the Child Abuse Potential Inventory. *Journal of Consulting and Clinical Psychology, 54,* 865-866.

Milner, J. S., & Robertson, K. R. (1989). Inconsistent response patterns and the prediction of child maltreatment. *Child Abuse & Neglect, 13,* 59-64.

Milner, J. S., & Robertson, K. R. (1990). Comparison of physical child abusers, intrafamilial sexual child abusers, and child neglecters. *Journal of Interpersonal Violence, 5,*
37-48.

Milner, J. S., Robertson, K. R., & Rogers, D. L. (1990). Childhood history of abuse and
adult abuse potential. *Journal of Family Violence, 5,* 15-34.

Milner, J. S., & Wimberley, R. C. (1979). An inventory for the identification of child
abusers. *Journal of Clinical Psychology, 35,* 95-100.

Milner, J. S., & Wimberley, R. C. (1980). Prediction and explanation of child abuse.
Journal of Clinical Psychology, 36, 875-884.

Mollerstrom, W. W., Patchner, M. A., & Milner, J. S. (1992). Family functioning and
child abuse potential. *Journal of Clinical Psychology, 48,* 445-454.

National Committee for Prevention of Child Abuse (NCPCA). (1992). *Evaluation of the
William Penn Foundation child abuse prevention initiative.* Chicago: Author.

Nealer, J. B. (1992). A multivariate study of intergenerational transmission of child
abuse (Doctoral dissertation, Ohio State University, 1992). *Dissertation Abstracts
International, 53,* 1848A.

Nunnally, J. C. (1978). *Psychometric theory.* New York: McGraw-Hill.

Osborne, Y. H., Williams, H. S., Rappaport, N. B., & Tuma, J. M. (1986, March). *Potential
child abusers: Deficits in childrearing knowledge and parental attitudes.* Paper presented at
the meeting of the Southeastern Psychological Association, Atlanta, GA.

Paulson, M. J., Afifi, A. A., Chaleff, A., Thomason, M. L., & Liu, V. Y. (1975). An MMPI
scale for identifying "at-risk" abusive parents. *Journal of Clinical Child Psychology,
4,* 22-24.

Paulson, M. J., Afifi, A. A., Thomason, M. L., & Chaleff, A. (1974). The MMPI: A
descriptive measure of psychopathology in abusive parents. *Journal of Clinical
Psychology, 30,* 387-390.

Poteat, G. M., Grossnickle, W. F., Cope, J. G., & Wynne, D. C. (1990). Psychometric
properties of the Wife Abuse Inventory. *Journal of Clinical Psychology, 46,* 828-834.

Pruitt, D. L. (1983). A predictive model of child abuse: A preliminary investigation
(Doctoral dissertation, Virginia Commonwealth University, 1983). *Dissertation
Abstracts International, 44,* 3206B.

Pruitt, D. L., & Erickson, M. T. (1985). The Child Abuse Potential Inventory: A study
of concurrent validity. *Journal of Clinical Psychology, 41,* 104-111.

Robertson, K. R., & Milner, J. S. (1983). Construct validity of the Child Abuse Potential
Inventory. *Journal of Clinical Psychology, 39,* 426-429.

Robertson, K. R., & Milner, J. S. (1985). Convergent and discriminant validity of the
Child Abuse Potential Inventory. *Journal of Personality Assessment, 49,* 86-88.

Robitaille, J., Jones, E., Gold, R. G., Robertson, K. R., & Milner, J. S. (1985). Child abuse
potential and authoritarianism. *Journal of Clinical Psychology, 41,* 839-843.

Schellenbach, C. J., Monroe, L. D., & Merluzzi, T. V. (1991). The impact of stress on
cognitive components of child abuse potential. *Journal of Family Violence, 6,* 61-80.

Schneider, C. J. (1982). The Michigan Screening Profile of Parenting. In R. H. Starr
(Ed.), *Child abuse prediction: Policy implications* (pp. 157-174). Cambridge, MA:
Ballinger.

Steele, B. F., & Pollock, C. B. (1974). A psychiatric study of parents who abuse infants
and small children. In R. E. Helfer & C. H. Kempe (Eds.), *The battered child* (2nd ed.,
pp. 92-139). Chicago: University of Chicago Press.

Straus, M. A., & Gelles, R. J. (1990). *Physical violence in American families*. New Brunswick, NJ: Transaction Books.

Stringer, S. A. (1983). A study of mothers and children at risk for child abuse (Doctoral dissertation, University of Miami, 1982). *Dissertation Abstracts International, 43,* 2369B.

Stringer, S. A., & La Greca, A. M. (1985). Correlates of child abuse potential. *Journal of Abnormal Child Psychology, 13,* 217-226.

Thomasson, E., Berkovitz, T., Minor, S., Cassle, G., McCord, D., & Milner, J. S. (1981). Evaluation of a family life education program for rural "high risk" families. *Journal of Community Psychology, 9,* 246-249.

Touliatos, J., Perlmutter, B. F., & Straus, M. A. (1990). *Handbook of family measurement techniques*. Newbury Park, CA: Sage.

Tzeng, O., Jackson, J., & Karlson, H. (1991). *Theories of child abuse and neglect: Differential perspectives, summaries, and evaluations*. New York: Praeger.

Vogel, A. M. (1987). The efficacy of a Head Start educational program for parents identified as potential abusers (Doctoral dissertation, Kansas State University, 1987). *Dissertation Abstracts International, 48,* 2515A.

Whissell, C., Lewko, J., Carriere, R., & Radford, J. (1990). Test scores and sociodemographic information as predictors of child abuse potential scores in young female adults. *Journal of Social Behavior and Personality, 5,* 199-208.

Wolfe, D. A. (1988). Child abuse and neglect. In E. J. Mash & L. G. Terdal (Eds.), *Behavioral assessment of childhood disorders* (2nd ed., pp. 627-669). New York: Guilford.

Wolfe, D. A., Edwards, B., Manion, I., & Koverola, C. (1988). Early intervention for parents at risk of child abuse and neglect: A preliminary investigation. *Journal of Consulting and Clinical Psychology, 56,* 40-47.

4

Prediction of Wife Assault

Daniel G. Saunders

A woman asks her counselor whether her fiancé is someday likely to abuse her. He recently told her that his father had beaten him severely as a child. She also suspects that his abuse of alcohol is more serious than he lets on.

A judge wonders whether she should sentence an assaultive husband to a treatment program. Several years ago the man was imprisoned for selling drugs, and he made a mockery of the prison's treatment programs.

An intake counselor at a domestic abuse program asks his supervisor whether a man he is assessing should be treated immediately or wait a month for group treatment. The man has been violent outside the home, including fights with friends and police officers when he was drunk. His wife called to say that she does not feel safe staying at her mother's house—he once came through a window there and knocked her mother down in his attempt to find her.

These are just some of the types of situations practitioners routinely face that call for the prediction of domestic violence. Although the science of predicting wife assault is quite inexact, practitioners frequently make informal risk assessments of future violence (Gottfredson & Gottfredson, 1988). In some situations they are legally mandated to assess imminent danger and to attempt to avert a tragedy. As domestic abuse programs work more closely with criminal justice agencies, their staff increasingly will be asked to make formal predictions. Thus, although the "state of science" in this area is imprecise, practitioners need the best information available.

The purpose of this chapter is to provide the latest scientific information on risk factors for wife assault and the clinical assessment of these factors. Special attention is given to predicting serious assault because of its severe consequences, including the possibility of homicide. Other types of prediction also are covered: What factors are related to recidivism after abuser treatment? When child custody is decided, is the abuser or his partner at more risk for abusing the children? What are the odds that a man who batters will be violent in a new relationship? Prediction in this area has many important applications—in sentencing, probation work, and treatment. Examples of these applications are given.

When the terms *wife* and *marital* are used, unless otherwise noted they refer to cohabiting relationships as well. Major studies of risk factors combined cohabiting and married cases. Risk factor research on dating violence is less well developed and has been reviewed elsewhere (Sugarman & Hotaling, 1991).

❏ Review of Risk Markers

A review of risk markers is given for various types of domestic assault. We cannot say for certain whether a risk marker is a causal predictor. The first step in developing a predictive model is often the uncovering of factors associated with a phenomenon (Mercy & O'Carroll, 1988). These markers may simply co-occur with the abuse. Or they may precede the abuse, but only because they are related to a true causal factor. Longitudinal studies provide stronger evidence of causal connections, but these studies are rare in the field of domestic violence. Therefore care is taken in this review to primarily use the terms *risk marker* or *risk factor* instead of *predictor*. From a practical standpoint, however, risk markers still may be useful in alerting practitioners when to expect violence or what type to expect.

Homicide is the most difficult to predict because it is rare.

The science of predicting violence may never be very good, especially for violence that is infrequent. This imprecision is simply a matter of the difficulty in predicting rare events. The problem we face is that serious forms of violence are generally the least frequent. Homicide, for example, is the most difficult to predict because it is rare, compared with other violence, yet it is the behavior that is likely to concern us most (see Sherman, 1992, for discussion). This review begins with the more common forms of domestic violence before turning to its severe forms.

RISK FACTORS FOR ASSAULT

Our knowledge of what distinguishes assaultive from nonassaultive men has grown steadily in the past decade. Recent reviews of the empirical literature document the existence of a number of risk factors that are found consistently across studies (Hotaling & Sugarman, 1986; Tolman & Bennett, 1990). The findings, however, should not obscure the possibility that men who batter may not be too different from other men. Men who batter may be at one end of a continuum of male socialization.

Risk factors that are found most consistently are presented first, followed by those showing less consistency. No attempt is made to place these factors into a detailed theoretical framework.

Violence in Family of Origin. As one might expect, men who batter experienced family violence in their childhoods. There may be a somewhat stronger effect for witnessing violence than for being its target (Hotaling & Sugarman, 1986). Even so-called minor violence or punishment against boys is a risk factor for them becoming domestically assaultive (Straus, 1980). Men who both witnessed violence and suffered directly from it are even more likely to be domestically violent. Social learning theory may provide the most parsimonious explanation for this intergenerational transmission, but it is not the only plausible explanation.

Demographic Factors. Although wife assault cuts across all socioeconomic groups, it is more prevalent among men with lower incomes and less education (Hotaling & Sugarman, 1986). Differences between the demographics of the partners also appear to place the men at risk. For example, differing religious backgrounds was a risk marker in all three studies that investigated this factor (Hotaling & Sugarman, 1986). The woman's greater education or occupational status was a risk factor in most studies, possibly because her status threatened the patriarchal beliefs of the man. This was not as prominent a risk factor as other demographics, but it is one that is extremely easy for the practitioner to uncover.

Alcohol. High rates of alcohol use or alcoholism appear characteristic of most abusers. Tolman and Bennett (1990) calculated the percentage of chronic alcohol abusers or alcoholics across 13 studies of batterers to be nearly 60% (median). Intoxication at the time of the violence is less clearly a risk marker. Coleman and Straus's (1983) findings suggest that severe intoxication may decrease violence.

Behavioral Deficits. Several researchers have found that men who batter report being less assertive than other men (Douglas, Alley, Daston, Svaldi-Farr, & Samson, 1984; Maiuro, Cahn, & Vitaliano, 1986; Rosenbaum & O'Leary, 1981). In one study the men were assertive in saying no to requests but were not adept at "initiating" forms of assertiveness (Maiuro et al., 1986). Dutton and Strachan (1987) found that low verbal assertion was related to violence in men with the greatest need for power. This need probably produced greater anger and anxiety in them, and violence erupted when they did not have the skills to handle their feelings. Margolin and her associates (Margolin, John, & Gleberman, 1988) observed couples interact and found some behavioral excesses by violent husbands: They had more negative voice qualities and more signs of irritation and frustration.

Psychopathology. The magnitude of the problem of woman abuse and the evidence for sociocultural factors has minimized attention to psychopathology. Although only a small percentage of abusers appear to have severe mental disorders, broad definitions of psychopathology may be applicable to most abusers (e.g., Axis II disorders). Most abusers in treatment programs show clinical elevations on at least some of the subscales of the Millon Clinical Multiaxial Inventory (MCMI) (Millon, 1983) and the Minnesota Multiphasic Personality Inventory (MMPI) (Coates, Leong, & Lindsey, 1987; Hamberger & Hastings, 1986). Profiles of psychological tests match clinical impressions of the men (Bernard & Bernard, 1984; Schuerger & Reigle, 1988). One average MMPI profile described the abuser as distrustful of others, isolated, and feeling insecure and alienated. The men maintain a strong masculine identification although they may be excessively concerned about their own masculinity (Bernard & Bernard, 1984). No consistent profile has been found on the MCMI (Hamberger & Hastings, 1986). Pathology may be related to alcoholism because one study found that alcoholic batterers were most likely to have clinical elevations on the MCMI (Hamberger & Hastings, 1991). Chronic alcohol abuse, for example, could lead to paranoia.

> *Surveys show that about half of the men who batter their wives also batter their children.*

Violence Toward Children. Both random and nonrandom surveys consistently show that about half of the men who batter their wives also batter their children (Saunders, 1994). Most studies defined violence toward the children as more severe than a slap or a spanking. In the random survey by Straus (1983), 50% of the violent husbands and 7% of the nonviolent husbands abused their children.

Battered women are also above normal risk for abusing their children, but it is much lower than the risk that the men will do so. The women's violence seems to be situationally related, whereas the men's abuse of the children seems related to chronic problems such as alcohol abuse and their own childhood traumas (Saunders, 1994).

Anger. Anger and hostility are not consistently related to violence. The type of measure may explain this inconsistency. The Buss-Durkee Hostility Inventory (Buss & Durkee, 1957) and responses to videotapes of women "engulfing" or "abandoning" their partners reveal anger in domestic assaulters. Their anger does not necessarily exceed that of nondomestic assaulters (reviewed in Tolman & Bennett, 1990). When anger is measured on the Novaco Anger Index (Novaco, 1975), a measure of situations likely to evoke anger, men who batter do not score above the norm. When this index is modified to be maritally specific, it is related to aggressive behavior reported by the women (Saunders & Hanusa, 1986). Thus the type of situation makes a difference, consistent with the feminist view that women are the targets of men's displaced anger or that anger erupts when women break the rules of patriarchy.

Stress. Like anger, stress does not appear to be consistently related to violence (Hotaling & Sugarman, 1986). Some evidence suggests that men's work stress is a risk factor (Barling & Rosenbaum, 1986). Studies that show a link between "external stress" and violence (e.g., Straus, 1980) are difficult to interpret because many of the items may be the result, rather than the cause, of violence. For example, items like "divorce," "separation," and "problems with the boss" are likely to be the direct result of aggressive behavior, and not their cause.

Depression and Low Self-Esteem. The causal role of depression is also difficult to decipher. Men who batter generally appear to score above the norm on standard measures of depression (Tolman & Bennett, 1990) and in one study were more depressed than nondomestic assaulters (Maiuro et al., 1986). However, their depression may be the result of the arrest and separation that often precede treatment. Some evidence shows that batterers who are not publicly detected are not depressed (Hamberger & Hastings, 1990).

Although related to depression, self-esteem may not respond to situational losses and stress as much as measures of depression. Three of the five studies reviewed by Hotaling and Sugarman (1986) showed that men who batter suffered from low self-esteem.

Nonrisk Factors. Researchers have been surprised to find that traditional sex role attitudes have not distinguished batterers from nonbatterers. At least six studies have had nonsignificant results (Hotaling & Sugarman, 1986). One explanation is that only some types of batterers have traditional attitudes. Evidence for this explanation is presented later.

The majority of studies also have not found evidence that these men have greater decision-making power in the relationship or a need for power. The largest and most representative study, however, does show power imbalance to be a risk marker (Straus, Gelles, & Steinmetz, 1980). The factor may be important also for only a subset of abusers; for example, one study found it to be a factor for blue-collar men with few "resources" (Allen & Straus, 1980). Another study found that men's perceived powerlessness was associated with violence (Babcock, Waltz, Jacobson, & Gottman, 1993). Cross-cultural studies clearly indicate patriarchal norms and sexual inequality as risk factors (Levinson, 1989; Yllö, 1983).

Concomitants. Some factors may be seen frequently in conjunction with abuse but are probably concomitants, rather than useful risk factors. For example, marital distress and arguments and conflict in the relationship are often associated with violent relationships (O'Leary & Vivian, 1990; Straus et al., 1980). Sexual assault often co-occurs with physical abuse as well (Hotaling & Sugarman, 1986).

Summary. Table 4.1 lists the risk factors described above and labels them as "prominent," "probable," or "possible," according to the strength of evidence supporting them. The table also lists characteristics of the severe assaulter, to be described later. Many of the studies reviewed used samples of men in treatment, and thus the findings may not apply to other men.

PREDICTION OF CONTINUANCE OF VIOLENCE

The factors reviewed in the above section are for the occurrence of wife assault, whether it is the first time it occurs or is repeated. Most wife assault is repeated—about two thirds of assaulters repeating their violence in 1 year, averaging about 6 times (Straus et al., 1980). In a study of police reports, 20% of the couples accounted for nearly half of all incidents (Sherman, 1992). Little is known about risk factors

Table 4.1 Risk Factors for Wife Assault

Risk Factor	Degree of Risk Any Assault	Severe Assault	Comments
Violence in family of origin	a	a	More risk if man both saw abuse and was abused
Low education and income of man	a		More risk if woman higher status
Alcohol	a	a	Chronic abuse may be key factor
Behavioral deficits	b		Especially if combined with need for power
Personality disorders	b		Wide variety of patterns and disorders
Child abuse	b	c	Half of violent husbands severely abuse a child
Anger	b		Especially for marital situations
Stress	c		"Stressor" may be the result of violence
Depression	c		Low self-esteem may be better risk marker
Generalized aggression		a	Violent both inside and outside the home
Antisocial traits		c	Criminal lifestyle and no remorse for violence

a = prominent risk; b = probable risk; c = possible risk.

for single occurrences versus repeated abuse. Two studies asked women about the characteristics of the first and subsequent episodes of violence. Walker (1984) found that, over time, (a) assaults were more likely to occur in public settings (from 17% to 40%), (b) more victims sensed the assaults would happen (from 13% to 48%), and (c) the men were less likely to justify or apologize after the abuse (from 82% to 59%). Women interviewed by Giles-Sims (1983) reported that certain events were linked with the first episode: pregnancy, illness, a new job for the woman, a move, or a divorce from another partner. Such events were less likely for the most recent episode, in which the man's job loss or job stress seemed to be the precipitant. Murphy and O'Leary (1989), in their longitudinal study, found that verbal aggression early in the relationship was a risk factor of the first instance of physical aggression. This verbal aggression was preceded by personality traits of defensiveness and aggressiveness (O'Leary, Malone, & Tyree, 1994).

Carmody and Williams (1987) found little difference between one-time and repeat offenders in the offenders' perceptions of abuse consequences. The repeat offenders were somewhat less likely to view arrest and social condemnation as severe consequences. It is unknown, however, whether these views were related to repeating violence or experience taught them that the consequences were slight.

Once a violent man leaves his partner, it does not mean that his violence ends. Evidence suggests that many find new partners to abuse. In two nonrandom studies that investigated this issue, the majority of men were abusive in more than one relationship (86% [Ganley & Harris, 1978]; 57% [Pagelow, 1981]). Many of the men also harass and abuse their ex-partners—anywhere from one fourth to two thirds of the cases, depending on the study (Epstein & Marder, 1986; Kelso & Personette, 1985; Saunders & Size, 1980).

RISK FACTORS FOR SEVERE WIFE ASSAULT

Wife assault varies greatly in its degree of severity, and many practitioners are interested in making predictions of severe assault. In most studies *severe assault* refers to violence that is often life-threatening and includes beatings, hitting with an object, and use of weapons. The smaller size and lesser strength of women mean that acts that may not have serious consequences when committed by a woman (e.g., hitting with an object) are likely to be serious when committed by a man (Saunders, 1988).

Risk factors for severe domestic assault can be derived from studies on types of men who batter. Most of these studies include severe assault as a variable. These studies point consistently to three risk factors for severe assault: generalized aggression, alcohol abuse, and abuse by parents.

Generalized Aggression. The severe domestic assaulter is likely to be violent outside the home, as well as inside (Fagan, Stewart, & Hansen, 1983; Gondolf, 1988; Hanneke & Shields, 1983; Saunders, 1992a).

This violence may be against relatives or strangers. Reports of this violence can be gathered rather easily from offenders or victims; arrest records also can be used. Offenders do not appear to distort their responses when asked about arrest history (Saunders, 1991).

Alcohol Abuse. Alcohol abuse is associated with severe domestic abuse (Brisson, 1981; Eberle, 1982; Fagan et al., 1983; Gondolf, 1988; Saunders, 1992a; Snyder & Fruchtman, 1981). The studies showing this association measured alcohol abuse as a general problem or alcohol involvement in violent incidents. The studies used victim or offender reports. One study did not find an association with alcohol abuse, but did for help sought for alcohol and drug problems (Shields, McCall, & Hanneke, 1988). In a study of dating violence, Makepeace (1988) showed that the amount of alcohol consumed prior to the violence was related to injury severity. Drug use was associated with severe assault in two studies (Gondolf, 1988; Shields et al., 1988). One study found a negative relationship between "alcohol/drugs involved" and severe violence; however, the severe violence was limited to only the severest episode (Bowker, 1983). Observations by police officers also showed a negative relationship between alcohol use and injuries (Bard & Zacker, 1974; Zacker & Bard, 1977); however, the police presence may have prevented an assault.

Abuse by Parents. The majority of studies have found that if the man as a child was abused by his parents, he is more likely to be severely violent in his marriage (Fagan et al., 1983; Hofeller, 1980; Saunders, 1994; Shields et al., 1988). Only the study by Bowker (1983) did not find this relationship. Most of the studies defined childhood abuse vaguely but implied or stated that it was severe abuse (more than a spank or a slap). Thus the distinction between childhood abuse as a risk marker for all domestic assault and severe domestic assault may be related to the severity of childhood abuse.

Abuse by parents may be related to generalized violence and to alcohol abuse. Social learning theory predicts that childhood victimization may lead to aggression toward others. A trait of aggressiveness may develop, just as there appears to be a trait of anger (Spielberger, Jacobs, Russell, & Crane, 1983). Aggressive patterns established in childhood appear to be stable over time (Olweus, 1979). Childhood victimization also may produce post-traumatic stress disorder (PTSD) in batterers (Dutton, 1988). Alcohol may be used to deaden the pain of childhood traumas. This use is consistent with the finding that anger and other emotions are not extremely high in the severe assaulter (Saunders, 1992a). Alcohol abuse and dissociative states may contribute to "deindividuated violence" in the severe assaulter. Dutton (1988) describes this violence as escalating to the point of frenzy, unresponsive to the pleading of the victim, and ending only when the abuser is exhausted.

Other Factors. Other factors have been studied less often but appear consistent with the above risk factors. Taken as a whole, these factors portray the severe abuser as having an antisocial personality. The range of violence of the severe abuser also seems to be greater. The violence is more likely to include sexual abuse (Bowker, 1983; Campbell, 1989; Gondolf, 1988; Snyder & Fruchtman, 1981) and to occur while the woman is pregnant (Bowker, 1983). Two out of three studies also found the wife abusers were more likely to abuse the children (Bowker, 1983; Gondolf, 1988; Snyder & Fruchtman, 1981).

Severely violent abusers appear to be involved in a criminal lifestyle, including robbery (Gondolf, 1988) and gambling (Shields et al., 1988). They are more likely to blame the victim for the abuse, to justify their violence, and to show no remorse (Gondolf, 1988; Hofeller, 1980; Shields et al., 1988). They seem to have more traditional sex role beliefs (Saunders, 1992a), but evidence for their dominant behavior is inconsistent (Hofeller, 1980; Saunders, 1992a). Their attitudes may be reinforced by friends because indications are they have more contact with friends than other abusers (Bowker, 1983).

Severe assaulters are likely to have more separations and divorces (Bowker, 1983; Gondolf, 1988; Shields et al., 1988). Other demographic factors are not so consistently present. Studies suggest that severe abusers are younger, have less stable residences, and have partners with low incomes (Bowker, 1983). Low income also was found among these men in the second national study of family violence (Hotaling & Sugarman, 1990). In two studies, less educated men were the severest assaulters (Bowker, 1983; Shields et al., 1988), but these and other demographic factors (e.g., race, income) did not characterize the severe assaulters in other nonrandom studies (Gondolf, 1988; Saunders, 1992a).

In summary, severe assault is linked most closely with severe childhood abuse, patterns of generalized aggression, and alcohol abuse. "Antisocial" seems an apt label because of the severe assaulters' lack of remorse for the abuse and involvement in other types of crime. Table 4.1 presents a summary of the risk factors for severe assault and shows the risk factors in common with assaults in general. Straus (1993) also recently reviewed studies of severe assault and constructed a list of risk factors. He recommends that research be conducted on combinations of factors that most accurately predict severe violence. Severe assaulters appear to be the "undercontrolled hostility" type of offender described by Megargee (1982), as opposed to the "overcontrolled" offender who restricts his violence to the home. Hershorn and Rosenbaum (1991) found that two types of hostility could differentiate groups of men who batter. Although there is some consistency in the above studies, they warrant cautious interpretation because most of the samples were nonrepresentative.

RISK FACTORS FOR FREQUENT ASSAULT

The severity of assaults is not strongly related to their frequency (see, e.g., Bowker, 1983; Snyder & Fruchtman, 1981). Therefore these dimensions need to be considered separately. Less is known about risk factors for frequency than for severity. The women in Snyder and Fruchtman's (1981) survey who experienced the most frequent violence also experienced the most threats (87%) and a high rate of marital rape (70%). The most frequently assaulted women in Bowker's (1983) study were less educated and had lower incomes. Their husbands had less education than other men and had mothers who did not work outside the home. These men were also more likely to have experienced and witnessed abuse in childhood. Alcohol/drug involvement before marriage was highly associated with assault frequency—more than the frequency of premarital violence and the wife's suspicion that the husband had a violent temper. Frequency of violence was related to pregnancy as a reason for marriage and the differing values each partner placed on children and dependency in the relationship.

Two studies combined verbal and physical abuse and also the frequency and severity dimensions by multiplying them together.

Schuerger and Reigle (1988) found that the magnitude of abuse was related to a number of factors in the men: being abused and witnessing abuse in childhood, lower education, irrational beliefs, anxiety, alcoholism, alienation, and social nonconformity. Rouse (1984) discovered that the magnitude of abuse was related to the observation of abuse but not to victimization in childhood. A low sense of personal efficacy also was related to the magnitude of abuse.

PREDICTION OF ASSAULT AFTER INTERVENTION

Once an intervention occurs with an assaulter, what are the risk factors for repeated assault? A few studies have attempted to answer this question. Studies show that, after arrest for misdemeanor assaults, without treatment at least 19% to 25% of the abusers will be violent again 6 to 12 months after arrest (Jaffe, Wolfe, Telford, & Austin, 1986; Sherman & Berk, 1984). Recidivism rates are lower in cases with no severe assault prior to arrest (Fagan, Friedman, Wexler, & Lewis, 1984). The impact of arrest may be because of its deterrent effects or because it teaches the men about current social norms (Dutton, 1988). There is good support for the notion that fear of divorce, social condemnation, and loss of self-respect are as important or more important than arrest to these men (Bowker, 1983; Dutton, 1988). One study showed that restraining orders did not relate to assault cessation, but did relate to less harassment in the less severe cases (Grau, Fagan, & Wexler, 1984).

Recidivism after specialized abuser treatment ranges in various studies from 28% to 45%, with an average of about 36% (Saunders & Azar, 1989). For men dropping out of treatment, the percentage is higher—about 52% on the average. Percentages vary across studies, probably because of different follow-up periods and definitions of abuse. For severe types of violence, evidence suggests that treatment adds significantly to the effects of arrest in stopping violence (Dutton, 1988).

Hamberger and Hastings (1990) contacted the men or their partners during the year after treatment. Reports of any form of violence were counted as recidivism. Recidivists were younger, reported alcohol to be a problem (especially after treatment), and were more narcissistic (as measured on the MCMI). DeMaris and Jackson (1987) surveyed men who attended at least one treatment session. The men who reported recidivism were more likely to have alcohol problems and exposure to their parents' violence in childhood. They were less likely to call a counselor if violence seemed imminent. Tolman and Bhosley (1991) found that successful cases had shorter histories of abuse. They found that criminal justice involvement predicted success, which Hamberger and Hastings (1990) did not find.

RISK FACTORS FOR TREATMENT ATTRITION

Many abusers who apply for treatment do not complete the assessment or treatment phases, as many as 56% in some studies (Grusznski & Carrillo, 1988). Knowing risk factors for attrition can help practitioners decide which men to keep from treatment or find ways to enhance their treatment motivation. Some simple demographic factors are related to dropping out of treatment—for example, lower education and income and being younger (DeMaris, 1989; Grusznski & Carrillo, 1988; Saunders & Parker, 1989). Legally mandated referrals seem to keep only some types of offenders in treatment, specifically those who are young and less educated (Saunders & Parker, 1989). Making threats prior to treatment, having an arrest record, and having fewer children are other risk factors for attrition in some studies (DeMaris, 1989; Grusznski & Carrillo, 1988).

❏ **Application of Risk Factor Research**

Risk factor research can be applied in a number of practice settings and for a variety of purposes. The growing realization that not all abusers are alike means that different interventions may be needed. The men differ in their propensity for violence inside and outside of marriage, for severe violence, and for successful cessation of violence after treatment.

In the first example at the beginning of the chapter, the counselor might advise the woman to suggest or even insist that her fiancé receive premarital counseling. The severe violence the man suffered in childhood and his problems with alcohol are poor risk markers for a violence-free marriage.

The judge has more of a quandary. Most research has focused on the effects of arrest rather than on jail sentences. Research on treatment efficacy is still in its infancy. More assessment of risk factors is needed in this case. Does this man have a drug abuse problem? Has he been violent outside the home? Was he raised in a violent home? The judge would do well to order the man to undergo simultaneous assessment at a program for men who batter and a drug treatment program. Both criminal justice sanctions and treatment are likely to be needed. Previous treatment may not have been successful for a number of reasons. For example, if it did not address childhood traumas that he experienced, he may not have learned the source of anger or ways to empathize with others. Rather than conclude that some offenders are untreatable, they simply may need more treatment or more treatment of a particular type. They may need repeated harsh consequences (e.g., jail or divorce) as well.

Probation and parole agents can use recidivism risk factors to determine what type of monitoring to provide. For example, because alcohol abuse is linked with recidivism, they may want to order random urine screens during and after treatment. In addition, they can assume that if a man has suffered severe childhood abuse, he may need long-term treatment to uncover and resolve the traumas. Agents can view such work as prevention of violence both inside and outside the home.

The intake counselor assessing the man who has been violent with police, friends, and his mother-in-law has good reason for concern. The man is separated from his partner, but that did not prevent him from finding her in the past. He needs immediate intervention for aggression and for alcohol abuse or dependency. A restraining order alone may not be effective in preventing his violence toward his partner or others (Elliott, 1989). Because this program, like many others, has a waiting list for its group treatment, innovations may be necessary. For example, "needier" clients can be linked immediately with a volunteer "sponsor"—a nonviolent man or reformed abuser (e.g., Almeida & Bograd, 1991). Marathon orientation groups also may provide immediate help and improve the chances the men will stay in treatment (Tolman & Bhosley, 1990).

❏ Methods of Prediction

Prediction of violence can be accurate only if reliable assessment tools are used. Fortunately many of the risk factors described above can be assessed from demographic and background information, rather than from sophisticated psychological tests. However, sensitive interview skills may be necessary for uncovering traumatic childhood events, drug abuse, and current patterns of violence.

ASSESSING VIOLENT BEHAVIOR

Most treatment programs use an expanded version of the Conflict Tactics Scale (CTS) (Straus, 1979). Items on sexual abuse, nonviolent threats, and use of the car as a weapon usually are added to the scale (Saunders, 1992b). One of these versions appears as Table 4.2. Because sexual abuse is such a sensitive area, questioning may need to be repeated over a number of sessions. Instructions for the scale focus on aggression arising from marital conflict, but these can be broadened to include any source of aggression. The full scale (not shown here) begins with positive behaviors and then shifts to verbal and then physical abuse. In this way psychological threat to the client is reduced. Other scales of spousal abuse have been developed, but they tend to focus on psychological abuse (Hudson & McIntosh, 1981; Lewis, 1985). Combining empathy for the man's feelings while confronting his behavior may help him open up (Saunders, 1982). For example, in the same session the worker can empathize with the man's hurt and anger over perceived or real criticism and also say directly that "hitting her was not okay."

The simplest time frame for the CTS includes the entire relationship. A much more complete picture is obtained with questions about the first, worst, and last episodes and about frequencies of each abusive behavior for a specific time frame, usually the past year. It is also important to ask about increases in severity and frequency because such increases are linked with life-threatening violence (Browne, 1987). An indicator of severity is the extent of injury, although many battered women do not sustain severe injuries. Pregnancy is not

Table 4.2 Woman Abuse Scale

The following is a list of things your partner may have done to you when you had an argument or at any other time. These are ways of being psychologically or physically abusive that people in our program often report. Please answer "yes" or "no" as to whether your partner behaved in each of these ways at any time in your relationship.

	Ever Happened?	
	Yes	No

Psychological Abuse

1. He did or said something to anger you	_____	_____
2. He sulked or refused to talk about an issue	_____	_____
3. He stomped out of the room, house, or yard	_____	_____
4. He insulted or swore at you	_____	_____
5. He interrupted your eating or sleeping	_____	_____
6. He said you could not leave to see certain people	_____	_____
7. He verbally pressured you to have sex	_____	_____
8. He made threats to leave the relationship	_____	_____
9. He made nonviolent threats to withhold money, take away the children, have an affair, etc.	_____	_____
10. He withheld sex from you	_____	_____
11. He screamed or yelled	_____	_____
12. He smashed, kicked, or hit an object	_____	_____

Physical Abuse

13. He threatened to hit you or throw something at you	_____	_____
14. He pushed, carried, restrained, grabbed, or shoved	_____	_____
15. He slapped or spanked you	_____	_____
16. He drove recklessly to scare you	_____	_____
17. He burned you	_____	_____
18. He threw an object at you	_____	_____
19. He kicked you or hit you with a fist	_____	_____
20. He threw you bodily	_____	_____
21. He physically forced sex on you	_____	_____
22. He hit you or tried to hit you with something	_____	_____

Life-Threatening Violence

23. He beat you up (multiple blows)	_____	_____
24. He choked or strangled you	_____	_____
25. He threatened you with a knife or gun	_____	_____
26. He used a knife or gun	_____	_____

Next, please tell how often each of these acts occurred from 1 year ago until today (response categories for each item):

once; twice; 3-5 times; 6-11 times (every other month); 12-24 times (1-2 per month); 25-36 times (2-3 per month); 37-52 times (3-4 per month); 53-104 times (1-2 per week); 105-156 times (2-3 per week); 157+ times (more than 3 per week)

SOURCE: Modified version of the Conflict Tactics Scale. From Straus (1979, p. 87). Reprinted with permission.

necessarily an inhibitor of aggression. In fact, pregnancy may increase the danger to the mother and unborn child (Gelles, 1988).

When possible, information on abusive behavior should be obtained from the victim. Studies consistently show that men underreport their violence (Saunders, 1992b). After treatment, the men show more agreement with their partners' reports (Edleson & Brygger, 1986).

The potential for imminent, severe danger has been assessed from the victims' viewpoint with a checklist of risk factors (Campbell, 1986). A list of indicators for use with offenders has been offered by McNeill (1987). The approach parallels that for suicide risk assessment. She suggests asking:

> the extent to which the client appears to have a plan, as distinguished from a fantasy
>
> the specificity with which the client describes the plan
>
> whether the client has targeted a victim or a victim is reasonably foreseeable with knowledge in the therapist's possession
>
> whether a dramatic or sudden change in the client's circumstances has occurred, such as divorce, loss of job, infidelity of spouse, romantic rejection, failure in an educational setting, humiliation caused by a known person, or death of a loved one
>
> whether any steps have been taken to execute the plan, such as purchasing a weapon or other dangerous material, buying an airplane ticket to visit the intended victim, saving money toward the objective, sending threats to the victim directly or through third parties, or performing minor acts as a prelude to the intended "grand finale"

ASSESSING RISK FACTORS FOR VIOLENCE

Violence in the family of origin can be assessed with the CTS. If time is too short for this scale, the most important factor to assess is whether severe abuse was witnessed or experienced.

Low education and income of the man are easy to assess, but it is also worth noting whether he is frustrated with his current status, for example, by asking, "Given your abilities and training, do you think you should have a better job?"

A history of generalized aggression can be obtained from the offender directly and supplemented with police and victim reports. The offender may be willing to disclose aggression toward friends and relatives during childhood that police and victims may not know about.

Alcohol abuse and dependency may best be evaluated by a specialist. Some standard measures can provide guidelines for initial screening. The Michigan Alcohol Screening Test (Selzer, 1971) is used widely but may not be adequate because it is related to help-seeking behavior and requires a great deal of openness. The Quantity-Frequency Index may provide more objective information because it relies on actual patterns of alcohol use (e.g., Fagan, Barnett, & Patton, 1988).

Rigid sex role beliefs and proviolence attitudes may be obvious from offender interviews or victim reports. Standard measures are available (e.g., Attitudes Toward Women Scale [Spence & Helmreich, 1978], Inventory of Beliefs About Wifebeating [Saunders, Lynch, Grayson, & Linz, 1987]). These measures can be faked easily, but adjustments can be made for social desirability response bias (Saunders, 1991).

Interview guides to use with the men and descriptions of other measures can be found elsewhere (Saunders, 1988, 1992b; Sonkin, Martin, & Walker, 1985). Computer-assisted assessment may be developed eventually, similar to procedures used for suicide risk assessment (Greist et al., 1973).

ASSESSING INHIBITORS TO VIOLENCE

The review of scientific literature indicated that fear of arrest may be only one inhibitor of future violence. Attempts also can be made to assess the man's fear of losing his partner and his self-respect. The scale used by Carmody and Williams (1987) provides a useful tool.

❑ Clinical Issues

In applying knowledge about prediction, some specific clinical issues arise. First, how much weight should be placed on clinical judgment or intuition, as opposed to statistically derived risk factors? Second, what ethical and legal issues are involved in predicting the most dangerous forms of violence? Third, how should predictions regarding particular cases be communicated within and among agencies?

INTUITIVE VERSUS STATISTICAL PREDICTION

Intuitive or "implicit" prediction makes use of the experience, knowledge, assumptions, and prejudices of decision makers (Morris & Miller, 1987). As certain as clinicians may be that their intuitive judgments are accurate, their track record in predicting violence is quite poor (Gottfredson & Gottfredson, 1986; Monahan, 1981). Statistical predictions based on known risk markers are also not very accurate, but they are more accurate than clinical judgments. Clinicians need to use statistically based methods of prediction because more than ever before they are *required* to make predictions of dangerousness. A major impetus for improved prediction has been a series of court decisions during the past 20 years finding clinicians negligent. The courts found that clinicians did not adequately predict dangerousness and subsequently did not warn and protect potential victims. Many are unaware that the most significant court cases, including the famous Tarasoff decisions, involved the killing of a girlfriend or a wife by her partner (McNeill, 1987). Thus clinicians in the domestic violence field must be armed with the best scientific knowledge. The prediction of dangerousness is not without its own dangers, however.

Ethical Concerns. Because predictive accuracy, even with statistical models, is not very high, some uses of prediction put civil liberties at risk. A difficult balancing act must be performed between protecting individual freedom and protecting society from harm (McFarlane, 1985). There seems to be less concern if predictions are used for short-term, emergency situations. For example, in the field of domestic violence, some jurisdictions may hold the assailant without bail for 24 hours. Most interventions for men who batter involve educational or treatment programs that use long jail sentences only rarely. Men typically attend weekly sessions for which they must pay some or all of the cost. More concern is likely to be raised about possible misuses of prediction if some men are sentenced to treatment that lasts two or three times that received by other men. The severest assaulters may need such long-term treatment, however (Saunders, 1992a).

Some uses of prediction put civil liberties at risk.

If treatment is seen as a form of punishment, some authors raise concerns about differential predictions. Morris and Miller (1987), for example, argue that "punishment should not be imposed, nor the term of punishment extended, by virtue of the use of predictions of dangerousness, beyond that which would be justified as a deserved punishment independent of that prediction" (p. 6). They warn that prediction can be used to decide who deserves special punitive or incapacitating treatment. Others stress that there can be utilitarian goals for prediction. It can be used to help rehabilitate or to deter (Gottfredson & Gottfredson, 1988).

A major ethical, and in some states statutory, obligation is to warn potential victims if they are in danger of severe violence. Threat to a specific individual is not an essential criterion for warning if the clinician can judge that a dangerous situation exists on the basis of the client's past behavior and present circumstances (McNeill, 1987). Counselors and clients need to be aware that confidentiality is not absolute. Clients need to be told at intake that confidentiality will not hold if they are in imminent danger of harming themselves or someone else. Clients who are feeling homicidal and making threats often feel comforted knowing that some controls will be placed on them, including the informing of law enforcement personnel and potential victims (McNeill, 1987).

Hart (1988) argues that simply warning victims does not offer them enough protection. She states that "all batterers' program policies and practices must specifically advance the safety interests of battered women and children" (p. 239).

An immediate, brief intervention for men entering treatment is the development of a "control plan" or "responsibility plan"—steps they will take to regulate anger and stop aggression. This plan includes not having access to weapons. Their partners should be informed of help available in the community, especially crisis services, and legal remedies should be explained to them. Victims should be told that offender treatment is not a "cure-all," that many batterers reoffend, and that victims may need continued reliance on the criminal justice system. Programs should evaluate the outcomes of their programs in order to provide overall recidivism data to the men's partners. The "safety checks" that some programs provide to women during and after treatment also can provide this recidivism data.

COMMUNICATION ABOUT DANGEROUSNESS
WITHIN AND AMONG AGENCIES

General information on the risk factors for assault, especially for frequent and severe assault, needs to be disseminated more widely. All practitioners having contact with assaulters and victims need this information. It is clear, for example, that many police officers lack knowledge of batterers' psychology. A man's demeanor in front of the police, which can be calm and rational, may not reflect his dangerousness. In the famous *Tarasoff* case, in which a woman was killed by her boyfriend, the doctors ordered the patient held for inpatient observation, but the police released the man because he promised not to go near her (McNeill, 1987).

Information on specific abusers may need to be shared among various professionals. Those who refer men for treatment, whether the criminal justice system or the victim, typically ask for little detailed information about treatment progress. They usually are given information about appropriateness for treatment, attendance, and overall compliance. Victims' reports of recurring abuse pose a number of dilemmas. For example, if a victim reports to her counselor that violence has recurred, should this information be shared with the offender's counselor? Some programs routinely share this information. Should the information be taken a step further to be used in confronting the offender? Because this use could put the victim at risk, the victim and the two counselors need to assess carefully whether and how the information should be used in the man's counseling.

Whether or not counselors working with men who batter receive reports directly from the men's partners, they would do well to have periodic contact with victim programs in order to be reminded of the controlling and aggressive tactics of the men and their tendency to minimize. Counselors need to view domestic violence as a crime and to be informed of the relevant civil and criminal statutes (Lerman & Cahn, 1991). Close contact with criminal justice agencies will keep one abreast of their policies. Many communities have task forces that develop a coordinated approach to the problem (Brygger & Edleson, 1987). Policies across agencies therefore can be made consistent. In some communities case conferences are held on particular families.

❏ Summary

At a time when practitioners in the domestic violence field are more aware of the need to predict accurately the most dangerous forms of violence, research is appearing that describes the most significant risk factors. Information on risk factors needs to be disseminated to direct service providers, as well as to policy makers. This chapter provides current information on risk factors for assault, especially severe and frequent assault, and for treatment attrition and recidivism. It describes tools for assessing violence and its correlates. Common clinical issues encountered in the field also are described. Those working in treatment and criminal justice settings need to realize that predictions cannot currently be made with any great certainty. Researchers one day may produce more precise prediction formulas that practitioners can use to avert tragedy.

❏ References

Allen, C. M., & Straus, M. A. (1980). Resources, power, and husband-wife violence. In M. A. Straus & G. T. Hotaling (Eds.), *The social causes of husband-wife violence* (pp. 188-210). Minneapolis: University of Minnesota Press.

Almeida, R. V., & Bograd, M. (1991). Sponsorship: Men holding men accountable for domestic violence. In M. Bograd (Ed.), *Feminist approaches for men in family therapy* (pp. 243-260). New York: Harrington Park.

Babcock, J. C., Waltz, J., Jacobson, N. S., & Gottman, J. M. (1993). Power and violence: The relation between communication patterns, power discrepancies, and domestic violence. *Journal of Consulting and Clinical Psychology, 61,* 40-50.

Bard, M., & Zacker, J. (1974). Assaultiveness and alcohol use in family disputes. *Criminology, 12,* 281-292.

Barling, J., & Rosenbaum, A. (1986). Work stressors and wife abuse. *Journal of Applied Psychology, 71,* 346-348.

Bernard, J. L., & Bernard, M. L. (1984). The abusive male seeking treatment: Jekyll and Hyde. *Family Relations, 33,* 543-547.

Bowker, L. H. (1983). *Beating wife-beating.* Lexington, MA: Lexington.

Brisson, N. (1981). Battering husbands: A survey of abusive men. *Victimology, 6,* 338-344.

Browne, A. (1987). *When battered women kill.* New York: Free Press.

Brygger, M. P., & Edleson, J. (1987). The Domestic Abuse Project: A multisystems intervention in woman battering. *Journal of Interpersonal Violence, 2,* 324-336.

Buss, A. H., & Durkee, A. (1957). An inventory for assessing different kinds of hostility. *Journal of Clinical and Consulting Psychology, 21,* 343-349.

Campbell, J. C. (1986). Nursing assessment of risk of homicide with battered women. *Advances in Nursing Science, 8,* 36-51.

Campbell, J. C. (1989). Women's responses to sexual abuse in intimate relationships. *Health Care for Women International, 8,* 335-347.

Carmody, D. C., & Williams, K. R. (1987). Wife assault and perceptions of sanctions. *Violence and Victims, 2,* 25-38.

Coates, C. J., Leong, D. J., & Lindsey, M. (1987, July). *Personality differences among batterers voluntarily seeking treatment and those ordered to treatment by the court.* Paper presented at the Third National Family Violence Research Conference, University of New Hampshire, Durham.

Coleman, D. H., & Straus, M. A. (1983). Alcohol abuse and family violence. In E. Gottheil, K. A. Druley, T. E. Skoloda, & H. M. Waxman (Eds.), *Alcohol, drug abuse, and aggression* (pp. 104-124). Springfield, IL: Charles C Thomas.

Demaris, A. (1989). Attrition in batterers' counseling: The role of social and demographic factors. *Social Service Review, 63*(1), 142-154.

Demaris, A., & Jackson, J. K. (1987). Batterers' reports of recidivism after counseling. *Social Casework, 68,* 458-465.

Douglas, M. A., Alley, J., Daston, A. P., Svaldi-Farr, J., & Samson, M. (1984, August). *Court-involved batterers and their victims: Characteristics and ethnic differences.* Paper presented at the 92nd Annual Convention of the American Psychological Association, Toronto.

Dutton, D. G. (1988). Profiling of wife assaulters: Preliminary evidence for a trimodal analysis. *Violence and Victims, 3,* 1, 5-29.

Dutton, D. G., & Strachan, C. E. (1987). Motivational needs for power and spouse-specific assertiveness in assaultive and nonassaultive men. *Violence and Victims, 2,* 145-156.

Eberle, P. A. (1982). Alcohol abusers and non-users: A discriminant analysis of differences between two subgroups of batterers. *Journal of Health and Social Behavior, 23,* 260-271.

Edleson, J. L., & Brygger, M. P. (1986). Gender differences in self-reporting of battering incidences. *Family Relations, 35,* 377-382.

Elliott, D. (1989). Criminal justice procedures in family violence crimes. In L. Ohlin & M. Tonry (Eds.), *Family violence* (pp. 427-480). Chicago: University of Chicago Press.

Epstein, M., & Marder, R. (1986). *Peace in the household: A follow-up study of battered women in Israel.* Unpublished report, U.S./Israel Women to Women.

Fagan, J., Friedman, E., Wexler, S., & Lewis, V. S. (1984). *National family violence evaluation: Final report. Vol. I: Analytic findings.* Unpublished manuscript, URSA Institute, San Francisco.

Fagan, J. A., Stewart, D. K., & Hansen, K. V. (1983). Violent men or violent husbands? Background factors and situational correlates. In D. Finkelhor, R. J. Gelles, G. T. Hotaling, & M. A. Straus (Eds.), *The dark side of families: Current family violence research* (pp. 49-68). Beverly Hills, CA: Sage.

Fagan, R. W., Barnett, O. W., & Patton, J. B. (1988). Reasons for alcohol use in maritally violent men. *American Journal of Alcohol and Drug Abuse, 14,* 371-392.

Ganley, A. L., & Harris, L. (1978, August). *Domestic violence: Issues in designing and implementing programs for male batterers.* Paper presented at the meeting of the American Psychological Association, Toronto.

Gelles, R. J. (1988). Violence and pregnancy: Are pregnant women at greater risk of abuse? *Journal of Marriage and the Family, 50,* 841-847.

Giles-Sims, J. (1983). *Wife battering: A systems theory approach.* New York: Guilford.

Gondolf, E. W. (1988). Who are those guys? Toward a behavioral typology of batterers. *Violence and Victims, 3,* 3, 187-204.

Gottfredson, D. M., & Gottfredson, S. D. (1988). Stakes and risks in the prediction of violent criminal behavior. *Violence and Victims, 3*(4), 247-262.

Gottfredson, S. D., & Gottfredson, D. M. (1986). The accuracy of prediction models. In A. Blumstein, J. Cohen, J. A. Roth, & C. A. Visher (Eds.), *Research in criminal careers and "career criminals"* (Vol. 2, pp. 212-290). Washington, DC: National Academy Press.

Grau, J., Fagan, J., & Wexler, S. (1984). Restraining orders for battered women: Issues of access and efficacy. *Women and Politics, 4,* 13-28.

Greist, J. H., Gustafson, D. H., Stauss, F. F., Rowse, G. L., Laughren, T. P., & Chiles, J. A. (1973). A computer interview for suicide risk prevention. *American Journal of Psychiatry, 130,* 1327-1332.

Grusznski, R. J., & Carrillo, T. P. (1988). Who completes batterer's treatment groups? An empirical investigation. *Journal of Family Violence, 3,* 141-150.

Hamberger, L. K., & Hastings, J. E. (1986). Personality correlates of men who abuse their partners: A cross-validation study. *Journal of Family Violence, 1*(4), 323-341.

Hamberger, L. K., & Hastings, J. E. (1990). Recidivism following spouse abuse abatement counseling: Treatment program implications. *Violence & Victims, 5,* 157-170.

Hamberger, L. K., & Hastings, J. E. (1991). Personality correlates of men who batter: Some continuities and discontinuities. *Journal of Family Violence, 6,* 131-147.

Hanneke, C. R., & Shields, N. M. (1983, July). *Patterns of family and nonfamily violence: An approach to the study of violent husbands.* Paper presented at the First National Conference for Family Violence Researchers, University of New Hampshire, Durham.

Hart, B. (1988). Beyond the "duty to warn": A therapist's "duty to protect" battered women and children. In K. Yllö & M. Bograd (Eds.), *Feminist perspectives on wife abuse* (pp. 234-248). Newbury Park, CA: Sage.

Hershorn, M., & Rosenbaum, A. (1991). Over- vs. undercontrolled hostility: Application of the construct to the classification of maritally violent men. *Violence and Victims, 6,* 151-158.

Hofeller, K. H. (1980). Social, psychological, and situational factors in wife abuse (Doctoral dissertation, Claremont Graduate School, 1980). *Dissertation Abstracts International, 41*(1-B), 408.

Hotaling, G. T., & Sugarman, D. B. (1986). An analysis of risk markers in husband to wife violence: The current state of knowledge. *Violence and Victims, 1,* 101-124.

Hotaling, G. T., & Sugarman, D. B. (1990). A risk marker analysis of assaulted wives. *Journal of Family Violence, 5,* 1-14.

Hudson, W. W., & McIntosh, S. R. (1981). The assessment of spouse abuse: Two quantifiable dimensions. *Journal of Marriage and the Family, 11,* 873-888.

Jaffe, P., Wolfe, D. A., Telford, A., & Austin, G. (1986). The impact of police charges on incidents of wife abuse. *Journal of Family Violence, 1,* 37-49.

Kelso, D., & Personette, L. (1985). *Domestic violence treatment services for victims and abusers.* Anchorage, AK: AWAIC.

Lerman, L. G., & Cahn, N. R. (1991). Legal issues in violence toward adults. In R. T. Ammerman & M. Hersen (Eds.), *Case studies in family violence* (pp. 73-86). New York: Plenum.

Levinson, D. (1989). *Family violence in cross-cultural perspective.* Newbury Park, CA: Sage.

Lewis, B. Y. (1985). The wife abuse inventory: A screening device for the identification of abused women. *Social Work, 30*, 32-36.

Maiuro, R. D., Cahn, T. S., & Vitaliano, P. P. (1986). Assertiveness deficits and hostility in domestically violent men. *Violence and Victims, 1*, 279-289.

Makepeace, J. (1988). The severity of courtship violence injuries and individual precautionary measures. In G. T. Hotaling, D. Finkelhor, J. T. Kirkpatrick, & M.A. Straus (Eds.), *Family abuse and its consequences: New directions in research* (pp. 297-311). Newbury Park, CA: Sage.

Margolin, G., John, R. S., & Gleberman, L. (1988). Affective responses to conflictual discussions in violent and nonviolent couples. *Journal of Consulting and Clinical Psychology, 56*, 24-33.

McFarlane, V. J. (1985). Clinical predictions on trial: A case for their defense. In C. D. Webster, M. H. Ben-Aron, & D. J. Hucker (Eds.), *Dangerousness: Probability and prediction, psychiatry and public policy* (pp. 209-225). London: Cambridge University Press.

McNeill, M. (1987). Domestic violence: The skeleton in Tarasoff's closet. In D. J. Sonkin (Ed.), *Domestic violence on trial: Psychological and legal dimensions of family violence* (pp. 197-217). New York: Springer.

Megargee, E. (1982). Recent research on overcontrolled and undercontrolled personality patterns among violent offenders. *Sociological Symposium, 9*, 37-50.

Mercy, J. A., & O'Carroll, P. W. (1988). New directions in violence prediction: The public health arena. *Violence and Victims, 3*, 285-301.

Millon, T. (1983). *Millon Clinical Multiaxial Inventory*. Minneapolis: National Computer Systems.

Monahan, J. (1981). *Predicting violent behavior. An assessment of clinical techniques.* Beverly Hills, CA: Sage.

Morris, N., & Miller, M. (1987, March). Predictions of dangerousness in the criminal law. *Research in Brief.* Washington, DC: U.S. Department of Justice, National Institute of Justice.

Murphy, C., & O'Leary, K. D. (1989). Psychological aggression predicts physical aggression in early marriage. *Journal of Consulting and Clinical Psychology, 57*, 579-582.

Novaco, R. W. (1975). *Anger control: The development and evaluation of an experimental treatment.* Lexington, MA: Lexington Books.

O'Leary, K. D., Malone, J., & Tyree, A. (1994). Physical aggression in early marriage: Prerelationship and relationship effects. *Journal of Consulting and Clinical Psychology, 62*, 594-602.

O'Leary, K. D., & Vivian, D. (1990). Physical aggression in marriage. In F. D. Fincham & T. N. Bradbury (Eds.), *The psychology of marriage: Basic issues and applications* (pp. 323-348). New York: Guilford.

Olweus, D. (1979). Stability of aggressive reaction patterns in males: A review. *Psychological Bulletin, 86*, 852-875.

Pagelow, M. D. (1981). *Woman-battering: Victims and their experiences.* Beverly Hills, CA: Sage.

Rosenbaum, A., & O'Leary, K. D. (1981). Marital violence: Characteristics of abusive couples. *Journal of Consulting and Clinical Psychology, 49*(1), 63-71.

Rouse, L. P. (1984). Models, self-esteem, and locus of control as factors contributing to spouse abuse. *Victimology, 9*(1), 130-141.

Saunders, D. G. (1982). Counseling the violent husband. In P. A. Keller & L. G. Ritt (Eds.), *Innovations in clinical practice: A source book* (pp. 16-29). Sarasota, FL: Professional Resource Exchange.

Saunders, D. G., (1988). Issues in conducting treatment research with men who batter. In *Coping with family violence: Research and policy perspectives* (pp. 145-157). Beverly Hills, CA: Sage.

Saunders, D. G. (1991). Procedures for adjusting self-reports of violence for social desirability bias. *Journal of Interpersonal Violence, 6,* 336-334.

Saunders, D. G. (1992a). A typology of men who batter wives: Three types derived from cluster analysis. *American Journal of Orthopsychiatry, 62,* 264-275.

Saunders, D. G. (1992b). Woman battering. In R. T. Ammerman & M. Hersen (Eds.), *Assessment of family violence: A clinical and legal sourcebook* (pp. 208-235). New York: John Wiley.

Saunders, D. G. (1994). Child custody decisions in families experiencing woman abuse. *Social Work, 39,* 51-59.

Saunders, D. G., & Azar, S. (1989). Family violence treatment programs: Descriptions and evaluation. In L. Ohlin & M. Tonry (Eds.), *Family violence: Crime and justice, a review of research* (Vol. 2, pp. 481-546). Chicago: University of Chicago Press.

Saunders, D. G., & Hanusa, D. R. (1986). Cognitive-behavior treatment of men who batter: The short-term effect of group therapy. *Journal of Family Violence, 1*(4), 357-372.

Saunders, D. G., Lynch, A. E., Grayson, M., & Linz, D. (1987). The inventory of beliefs about wife beating. *Violence and Victims, 2*(1), 39-57.

Saunders, D. G., & Parker, J. C. (1989). Legal sanctions and treatment follow-through among men who batter: A multivariate analysis. *Social Work Research and Abstracts, 25*(3), 21-29.

Saunders, D. G., & Size, P. B. (1980). *Marital violence and the police.* Research report to the Wisconsin Council on Criminal Justice, Madison.

Schuerger, J. M., & Reigle, N. (1988). Personality and biographic data that characterize men who abuse their wives. *Journal of Clinical Psychology, 44,* 75-81.

Selzer, M. (1971). The Michigan Alcoholism Screening Test: The quest for a new diagnostic instrument. *American Journal of Psychiatry, 127,* 1653-1658.

Sherman, L. W. (1992). *Policing domestic violence.* New York: Free Press.

Sherman, L. W., & Berk, R. A. (1984). The specific deterrent effects of arrest for domestic assault. *American Psychological Review, 49,* 261-272.

Shields, N. M., McCall, G. J., & Hanneke, C. R. (1988). Patterns of family and nonfamily violence: Violent husbands and violent men. *Violence and Victims, 3,* 83-97.

Snyder, D. K., & Fruchtman, L. A. (1981). Differential patterns of wife abuse: A data-based typology. *Journal of Consulting and Clinical Psychology, 49*(6), 878-885.

Sonkin, D. J., Martin, D., & Walker, L.E.A. (1985). *The male batterer: A treatment approach.* New York: Springer.

Spielberger, C. D., Jacobs, G. A., Russell, S., & Crane, R. S. (1983). Assessment of anger: The State-Trait Anger Scale. *Advances in Personality Assessment, 2* (J. N. Butcher & C. D. Spielberger, Eds.), 112-134.

Spence, J. T., & Helmreich, R. L. (1978). *Masculinity and femininity: Their psychological dimensions, correlates, and antecedents.* Austin: University of Texas.

Straus, M. A. (1979). Measuring family conflict and violence: The Conflict Tactics Scale. *Journal of Marriage and the Family, 41,* 75-88.

Straus, M. A. (1980). Victims and aggressors in marital violence. *American Behavioral Scientist, 23,* 681-704.

Straus, M. A. (1983). Ordinary violence, child abuse, and wife beating: What do they have in common? In D. Finkelhor, R. J. Gelles, G. T. Hotaling, & M. A. Straus

(Eds.), *The dark side of families: Current family violence research* (pp. 213-234). Newbury Park, CA: Sage.

Straus, M. A. (1993). Identifying offenders in criminal justice research on domestic assault. *American Behavioral Scientist, 36,* 587-600.

Straus, M. A., Gelles, R. J., & Steinmetz, S. K. (1980). *Behind closed doors: Violence in the American family.* Garden City, NY: Doubleday.

Sugarman, D. B., & Hotaling, G. T. (1991). Dating violence: A review of contextual and risk factors. In B. Levy (Ed.), *Dating violence: Young women in danger* (pp. 100-118). Seattle: Seal Press.

Tolman, R. M., & Bennett, L. W. (1990). A review of research on men who batter. *Journal of Interpersonal Violence, 5,* 87-118.

Tolman, R. M., & Bhosley, G. (1990). A comparison of two types of pregroup preparation for men who batter. In *Advances in group work research* (pp. 33-43). New York: Haworth.

Tolman, R. M., & Bhosley, G. (1991). The outcome of participation in a shelter-sponsored program for men who batter. In D. Knudsen & J. Miller (Eds.), *Abused and battered: Social and legal responses* (pp. 113-122). Hawthorne, NY: Aldine.

Walker, L. E. (1984). *The battered woman syndrome.* New York: Springer.

Yllö, K. (1983). Sexuality inequality and violence against wives in American states. *Journal of Comparative Family Studies, 14,* 67-86.

Zacker, J., & Bard, M. (1977). Further findings on assaultiveness and alcohol use in interpersonal disputes. *American Journal of Community Psychology, 88,* 153-160.

5

Prediction of Homicide of and by Battered Women

Jacquelyn C. Campbell

Homicide is the leading cause of death in the United States for African American women aged 15 to 34 (Farley, 1986). The rate of homicide per 100,000 for these young women was 20.0 in 1987, as compared with the overall rate of 8.5 per 100,000 for the entire U.S. population (Department of Health and Human Services, 1990). This rate is exceeded only by African American males (90.5 per 100,000) and Latino males (53.1 per 100,000) in the same age group (15 to 34 years). The homicide rate for African American women of all ages is higher than that of European American men (11.3 per 100,000 vs. 8.4 per 100,000), whereas the rate for European American women is 2.8 per 100,000. These rates translate to an average of 2,746 European

AUTHOR'S NOTE: Research reported in this chapter was supported by the National Center for Nursing Research, R29 #NR01678 (J. Campbell, Principle Investigator) and the Centers for Disease Control and Prevention, R49CCR #603514 (J. McFarlane and B. Parker, Principle Investigators).

American and 1,761 African American women killed each year (Farley, 1986). Other causes of death for females have been reduced since 1940, but death by homicide has increased for both European American and African American women. Data on Latina female homicide have only recently begun to be kept nationally.

❏ Homicide and Battering

Homicides involving women have different dynamics from those more often studied, between two males (Block, 1985; Daly & Wilson, 1988; Mercy & Saltzman, 1989). For example, 90% of women murdered are killed by men, men who are most often a family member, spouse, or ex-partner (Campbell, 1992; Wilbanks, 1986). Approximately 70% of murdered women are killed by a husband, lover, or estranged same. Approximately two thirds of those murdered by intimate partners or ex-partners had been physically abused before they were killed (Campbell, 1981, 1992; Wallace, 1986). Homicide of a female partner or ex-partner followed by suicide of the perpetrator is another form of homicide of women wherein a history of female battering is the most usual pattern (Humphrey, Hudson, & Cosgrove, 1981; Wallace, 1986).

Similarly, when women kill, they usually kill a family member. They most often kill husbands, ex-husbands, and lovers, and again there is a documented history of *wife* assault. Women are far more likely than men to kill during an incident when the victim was the first to commit a violent act, commonly termed *victim precipitation* in homicide research (Campbell, 1992; Daly & Wilson, 1988; Jurik & Winn, 1990; Mann, 1990).

> *When women kill, they usually kill a family member.*

❏ Need for Prediction

From these data it is clear that one of the major ways to decrease spousal homicide is to identify and intervene with battered women at risk for homicide. Recent research has demonstrated that the majority of battered women eventually leave their abusers (Campbell, Miller, Cardwell, & Belknap, 1994; Okun, 1986). The trajectory of abuse, however, is generally an increase in severity and frequency over time (Straus & Gelles, 1990) that may culminate in a homicide if the woman does not leave or the man does not receive either treatment or incarceration for violence. In addition, women are often highly at risk for homicide after they have left their abusers or when they make it clear to them that they are leaving for good (Daly & Wilson, 1988; Hart, 1988).

From in-depth interviews with battered women, it is clear that the majority carefully weigh the pluses and minuses of the overall relationship, both in terms of their safety and well-being and that of their children (Campbell et al., 1994). The majority, however, have not realistically appraised the potential for homicide. Even though many have thought about it, they may find it too frightening to dwell on. The possibility of reading in the paper that an abused woman seen in a research or therapeutic interaction has been killed is a constant concern to advocates and professionals. Advocates in wife abuse shelters are extremely concerned about women leaving the shelter without knowing how dangerous their situations might be. Thus clinicians who work with abused women need to make sure women realize the potential of homicide in their situation and to give them a way to realistically assess their risk of homicide. This is both an ethical and a legal imperative, as well as an aid to sleeping well at night (Hart, 1988).

For health care professionals, there is some similarity to explaining the risks of cancer to smokers so that they can make their own decisions about actions to be taken. Some analogies also can be made to the appraisal done for risk of suicide by physical and mental health care professionals wherein a clinical assessment is done, and if the risk is considered great, action is taken to ensure the person's safety. This type of unilateral professional action might come into play for an abused woman when her emotional trauma is so great that the professional believes she is unable to make reasonable decisions about her own safety. Yet the clinicians' "duty to warn" battered women about their risk of homicide, even though primarily a clinical issue, can be better informed by statistical prediction of dangerousness than by purely clinical suggestions.

The background on homicide of or by abused women presented above establishes the need for prediction. This chapter also includes a discussion of issues related to clinical prediction as contrasted with formal legal prediction and a description of the clinical lists of danger signs that have been published. These lists of warning signs for homicide in battering situations are based on research and clinical experience, but none have been subjected to psychometric testing. The chapter concludes with a presentation of the Danger Assessment instrument for prediction of homicide in battering relationships. Although predictive validity of the Danger Assessment has not been established, it is the only such instrument with any published empirical evaluation of psychometric properties (Campbell, 1986; Stuart & Campbell, 1989).

❑ Prediction Issues

Clinical prediction of dangerousness in situations of battering has legal implications. A series of court decisions during the past 20 years has held clinicians negligent for not adequately predicting dangerousness and subsequently for not at least protecting clients as potential victims and in some states for not providing warnings to potential victims of clients (Hart, 1988). General agreement by legal experts is that if a therapist decides that her or his patient is a serious danger to someone else, the therapist must warn potential victims (Small, 1985).

This legal mandate is especially pertinent where therapists are conducting couple counseling or treatment groups for batterers, because of the demonstrated risk of homicide in battering relationships. It places the onus of responsibility on the therapist for assessing for potential for homicide, as well as for warning potential victims. Therefore all couple counseling needs to include assessment for abuse done with each partner separately and, where abuse is found, assessment for homicide potential. Homicide

Ex-spouses also are known to be potentially lethal to their formerly abused female partners.

potential also needs to be assessed with men in batterer treatment groups whether or not they still are living with their partners. Ex-spouses also are known to be potentially lethal to their formerly abused female partners (Campbell, 1992). In both cases, where the clinician judges homicide potential to be high, both the abused partner and the police and/or parole officer need to be notified. In cases of high potential for homicide, the law is clear that the duty to warn takes precedence over confidentiality.

To determine the degree of homicide risk, clinicians usually make use of intuitive or clinical judgment prediction based on the clinician's training, experience, and expertise (see Chapter 2). This intuitive judgment also involves the implicit assumptions and prejudices of the clinician (Miller & Morris, 1988) and has a poor track record in accurate prediction of violence. Psychological testing that has been used in the patient's clinical assessment may improve the accuracy of clinical prediction. It also may be based on a reading of the literature or workshops that the clinician has attended on wife abuse. Some of that material contains lists of danger signals to watch for, signs that have been developed from a mixture of research results and clinical experience of the author or trainer. These lists can help prediction accuracy. Statistically based prediction using psychometrically developed instruments is not completely accurate either, especially in the instruments' present state of development in the area of spousal homicide, but is more so than clinical judgments.

The criminal justice system may use experts' predictions of homicide in battering situations in decisions about incarceration and/or court-mandated treatment of batterers. This use may be formal, as in court testimony, or informal, as in communication between a parole officer and the clinicians treating the batterer in the case. In fact, Straus (1991) presents an instrument that he recommends for determining dangerousness of abusive males as the basis for arrest decisions. The formal use of prediction for arrest and sentencing decisions demands as great a degree of accuracy as possible.

One of the most difficult prediction issues using instruments (statistical prediction) is cutoff scores. Instruments can have some psychometric validity in terms of construct validity without a good basis for determining scores that will predict accurately the occurrence of a homicide. Clinical advice given on matters of life and death probably would involve drastic measures by the client, and the clinician must be sure of the accuracy of any cutoff score. Only predictive validity testing, studies that determine the accuracy of the instrument in predicting actual homicide, gives a cutoff score that provides the kind of support necessary either to give clients definitive advice about avoiding a homicide or to advise the courts on the numerical probability of an abusive or abused partner committing homicide. At the time of writing this chapter, no instruments for predicting homicide in abusive relationships are available for which predictive validity information has been published. Therefore the use of cutoff scores is premature.

Prediction of homicide is especially difficult because homicide is even rarer than other forms of violence. Spousal homicide is even rarer and therefore even more difficult to predict. Because battering is the most frequent relationship precursor of spousal homicide, it makes sense to design a predictive instrument around characteristics related to abuse. Yet this design makes the number of occurrences, homicides in abusive relationships, even smaller. Thus research to establish future predictive validity will involve huge sample sizes and be enormously expensive and time consuming.

It would be important in any prediction of intimate relationship homicide study to include men and women who are dating and cohabiting and, especially important in terms of abusive relationships, to include ex-spouses and ex-cohabitors. Yet any such effort would be hampered by the well-known inaccuracies of national homicide files in terms of relationship category (Campbell, 1992; Wilson, 1991). The picture is confounded further because whether or not a serious assault becomes a homicide may be determined by the speed and/or quality of emergency response rather than by the relationship, perpetrator, and victim characteristics that can be measured and used for prediction. Finally, careful prediction validity assessment would be necessary to determine how various risk factors should be weighted. Common sense dictates that certain factors would be more predictive of homicide than others. Yet without a statistical evaluation, designation of which risk factors should be taken more seriously than others is also premature.

❏ **Published Lists of Danger Signs**

Sonkin, Martin, and Walker (1985) list weapons in the home, use of weapons in prior abusive incidents, threats with weapons, threats to kill, and serious (life-threatening) injury in prior abusive incidents under the homicide risk category in their batterer's assessment of lethality factors list (pp. 80-83). Thirteen other lethality factor categories also are listed: suicide risk, frequency/cycle of violence, history of violence, substance use/abuse, assaults on other family members, previous criminal history/activity, violence outside the home, isolation, proximity of victim and offender, attitudes toward violence, life stresses, general mental functioning, physical health, and therapist's evaluation. Each of the 13 categories is explained with further assessment probes, rather than as definitive risk factors. These authors recommend a therapeutic goal of lessening the risk of homicide or serious injury before addressing in-depth issues in treatment of abusers.

In Hart's (1988) treatise on the need to protect as well as warn battered women of potentially homicidal abusers, she also gives a list of factors to "be considered when assessing lethality" (p. 241): threats of homicide or suicide, fantasies of homicide or suicide, presence of weapons, obsessiveness about partner, centrality of battered woman (batterer is isolated from other support systems), rage, depression, drug or alcohol consumption, and access to the battered woman. Hart suggests that the first two factors are primary and the rest less important.

Straus (1991) based his list of "criteria for identifying life-threatening risk (LTR) among violent men" on the 1985 National Family Violence Survey. These criteria were associated with severe violence as measured on the Conflict Tactics Scale (CTS) (Straus & Gelles, 1990) and thus can be considered an instrument with concurrent construct validity support from one sample (although nationally representative). As well as three or more instances of violence in the previous year, Straus states that life-threatening risk from a male abuser is indicated by three or more of the following: He initiated two most recent instances of violence; wife needed medical treatment from abuse; police were involved in an incident in the previous 12 months; he was drunk more than three times a year, abused drugs in the past year, threatened to kill, threatened partner with a weapon in hand, owns a gun and threatens to use it; extreme male dominance or attempts to achieve such dominance; physical abuse of a child; thinks there are some situations when it is okay for a man to hit his wife; physically forced sex; extensive destruction of property; threats or actually killing or injuring a pet; history of psychological problems; assault of a nonfamily person or other violent crime; severe violence between parents; and verbally aggressive to partner (CTS verbal aggression score of 40+).

Thus the prediction risk factor lists reviewed so far concentrate on risk factors for male batterers killing their female partners. Although it happens slightly less often, abused women also kill their partners. Browne's (1987) list of factors that differentiated the battered women in her sample who killed their abusers from those who did not kill is often presented as a risk factor list. Although this list was developed from a concurrent predictive validity (ability to differentiate between groups) type study, it has not yet been substantiated in subsequent research with independent samples, nor have reliability or other forms of validity been assessed. The factors on this list are frequency of violent incidents, severity of injuries, man's threats to kill, woman's threats of suicide, man's drug use, man's frequency of intoxication, and forced sexual acts.

❏   Danger Assessment Instrument

The Danger Assessment (DA) instrument, presented in Figure 5.1, is considered to be a form of statistical prediction, as contrasted with clinical prediction, because it is based on prior research and has some preliminary evidence of reliability and validity. However, the instrument is considered to be most useful in clinical settings as a way to make clinical prediction more accurate. The items on the Danger Assessment have been established only as correlates of homicide, not directly causative factors. Therefore the instrument is best thought of as a statistical risk factor assessment, rather than as a prediction instrument per se. As such it could be used as a basis for discussion

with battered women by advocates in shelters, health care professionals in emergency rooms and primary care centers, and social
workers and psychologists in counseling situations. It could be used
also for informal prediction discussions with probation officers or
other officers of the court responsible for decisions about continuing
probation by those treating abusing men. As yet there are neither
cutoff scores nor weighting of items. It is not appropriate for formal
prediction as in court sentencing situations in its current state of
development.

DEVELOPMENT AND PSYCHOMETRIC
EVALUATION OF THE DANGER ASSESSMENT

Table 5.1 is a summary of the research in which formal instrument
evaluation assessments were made on the Danger Assessment. The
initial items on the instrument were developed from four retrospec-
tive research studies establishing risk factors in cases where battered
women were killed or seriously injured by their abusers or where
battered women killed or seriously injured their abusers (Berk, Berk,
Loseke, & Rauma, 1983; Browne, 1987; Campbell, 1981, 1992; Fagan,
Stewart, & Hansen, 1983). The initial instrument development study
(Study 1) was conducted with 79 abused women from the community recruited by newspaper advertisement and bulletin board post-
ings in two geographically and demographically distinct cities. Approximately 20% of that sample were from wife abuse shelters; 45.6%
of the sample were women of color; the mean educational level was
13.2 years of education; 38% had a total family income below poverty
level; and the mean age was 30.5 years. Scores on the instrument
ranged from 1 to 14, with a mean of 6.3. As shown in Table 5.1, mean
scores have ranged from 5.5 to 8.7 in samples of abused women. All
samples have included a substantial proportion of women of color
and have been from a variety of settings.

Part of both the shelter and hospital studies (2 and 3 [see Table 5.1])
was an open-ended interview section asking women their perception
of danger of being killed by their partners (Stuart & Campbell, 1989).
Women then were asked what made them believe they were in
danger or not. The majority of women perceiving a great amount of
danger in both studies mentioned choking as a tactic used against

Danger Assessment

Several risk factors have been associated with homicide (murder) of both batterers and battered women in research conducted after the killings have taken place. We cannot predict what will happen in your case, but we would like you to be aware of the danger of homicide in situations of severe battering and for you to see how many of the risk factors apply to your situation. (The *he* in the questions refers to your husband, partner, ex-husband, or whoever currently is physically hurting you.)

A. On the calendar, please mark the approximate dates during the past year when you were beaten by your husband or partner. Write on that date how long each incident lasted in approximate hours and rate the incident according to the following scale:

    1. Slapping, pushing; no injuries and/or lasting pain
    2. Punching, kicking; bruises, cuts, and/or continuing pain
    3. "Beating up"; severe contusions, burns, broken bones
    4. Threat to use weapon; head injury, internal injury, permanent injury
    5. Use of weapon; wounds from weapon

(If any of the descriptions for the higher number apply, use the higher number.)

B. Answer these questions yes or no.

_____ 1. Has the physical violence increased in frequency during the past year?

_____ 2. Has the physical violence increased in severity during the past year and/or has a weapon or threat with weapon been used?

_____ 3. Does he ever try to choke you?

_____ 4. Is there a gun in the house?

_____ 5. Has he ever forced you into sex when you did not wish to have sex?

_____ 6. Does he use drugs? (By drugs I mean "uppers" or amphetamines, speed, angel dust, cocaine, crack, street drugs, heroin, or mixtures.)

_____ 7. Does he threaten to kill you and/or do you believe he is capable of killing you?

_____ 8. Is he drunk every day or almost every day? (in terms of quantity of alcohol)

_____ 9. Does he control most or all of your daily activities? (For instance, does he tell you whom you can be friends with, how much money you can take with you shopping, or when you can take the car?) (If he tries but you do not let him, check here ___)

_____ 10. Have you ever been beaten by him while you were pregnant? (If never pregnant by him, check here ___)

_____ 11. Is he violently and constantly jealous of you? (For instance, does he say, "If I can't have you, no one can.")

_____ 12. Have you ever threatened or tried to commit suicide?

_____ 13. Has he ever threatened or tried to commit suicide?

_____ 14. Is he violent toward your children?

_____ 15. Is he violent outside the home?

_____ TOTAL YES ANSWERS

THANK YOU. PLEASE TALK WITH YOUR NURSE, ADVOCATE, OR COUNSELOR ABOUT WHAT THE DANGER ASSESSMENT MEANS IN TERMS OF YOUR SITUATION.

Figure 5.1. Danger Assessment

SOURCE: Copyright © 1985, 1988 by Jacquelyn Campbell, PhD, RN. Used by permission.

Table 5.1 Danger Assessment Research

	Studies				
	1	2	3	4	5
N	79 abused	30 abused	52 abused	156 mixed	164 relationship problem
Setting	80% community 20% shelter	shelter	36% ER 64% inpatient OB/GYN	Prenatal	Community
Ethnicity	46% minority	33% minority	62% minority	Black = 71 White = 46 Hispanic = 39	Black = 126 Nonblack = 37
Reliability	Alpha = .71	Test-retest = .94 Alpha = .60	Test-retest = .89 Alpha = .67	Alpha = .86	Alpha = .66
Validity	Construct (r) CTS = .55 Injury = .50 Tactic = .43	Construct (r) Injury = .48	None	Construct (r) ISA = .75 CTS = .49	Total sample (r) ISA-P = .66 ISA-NP = .44
$\overline{X}$	6.3	8.7	9.2 ER 8.3 inpatient OB/GYN	.3 not abused 3.5 abused Abused Black = 2.7 White = 4.4 Latino = 4.1	5.5

them that made them believe their partner might kill them. This item has been added to the scale and in subsequent evaluations affects neither the reliability nor the validity of the scale. Another item was added to the scale from the in-depth interview portion of the shelter study (2) that asked about the male partner's history of suicide threats and/or attempts. This item is related also to prior research on murder of abused women followed by suicide of the perpetrator (Humphrey et al., 1981). Addition of that item has slightly improved both the reliability and validity estimates.

Reliability

There is some controversy about whether internal consistency reliability is an appropriate psychometric technique to use with an instrument wherein each item is considered to be an independent risk factor. With no consensus in the literature on this issue, alpha coefficient internal consistency estimations on the instrument have been conducted, but they will tend to be low.[1] In the original study the alpha was .71. In subsequent studies it has ranged from .60 in a very small sample to .86 (see Table 5.1). In the two studies in which temporal stability (test-retest reliability) was assessed, it ranged from .89 to .94.

Validity

Convergent construct validity (positive relationships with similar constructs) of the instrument has been supported by correlations in the moderately strong range, with instruments measuring severity and/or frequency of abuse, the Conflict Tactics Scale (Straus & Gelles, 1990), the Index of Spouse Abuse (Hudson & McIntosh, 1981), and a rating of severity of worst injury incurred as a result of the abuse.

Validity in terms of differentiating groups (concurrent predictive validity) also is supported by the different means in the seven groups of abused women as seen in Table 5.1. These accurately reflect the differing degrees of severity of abuse one would expect in the different populations. The lowest scores were in the nonabused sample, with the next lowest in the prenatal sample, a group not known to be abused and expected to be early in an abuse pattern because of their relative youth and perhaps being protected from the worst of the abuse because of their pregnancy. In fact, very few women in this group reported increasing severity and/or frequency of battering during the pregnancy (McFarlane, Parker, Soeken, & Bullock, 1992). The highest scores were in the hospital emergency room group, a sample identified because of serious abuse-related injury. The next highest scores were from women in shelters, who often come to a shelter because of fear of a fatal incident. The samples of abused women from the community (Studies 1 and 5) had scores in the intermediary range.

INCREASING SEVERITY AND FREQUENCY OF BATTERING

The phenomenon of severity and frequency is assessed on the Danger Assessment by presenting the woman with a calendar of the past year. The woman is asked to mark the approximate days when physically abusive incidents occurred, to estimate the amount of time the incident lasted, and to rank the incident on the scale presented on the Danger Assessment (Figure 5.1). If she indicates the incidents occur weekly or more often than that, only 3 months of the calendar need to be filled out. Most women have no problem filling out the calendar; they remember these incidents very well.

In the original scale development, women were asked the first question about increase in severity and frequency, then were asked to fill out the calendar, and then were asked the question again on the basis of the calendar; 38% of the women who initially said there was no increase answered the question yes after filling out the calendar, thereby indicating that the calendar portion is an important part of the instrument despite its adding 8 to 10 minutes to the 6- to 8-minute basic administration time. In the two studies in which the calendar was not done (2 and 3), the first two items substantially lowered the internal consistency, also suggesting the efficacy of the calendar (Stuart & Campbell, 1989). From women's remarks as they complete the calendar, the calendar seems to function as a conscious-ness-raising exercise, helping to cut through the denial and minimi-zation that is a normal response to abuse (Ferraro & Johnson, 1983). Thus, using women's general recall of whether or not the abuse is increasing in severity and frequency as a predictor of homicide may not be entirely accurate without some sort of specific cuing such as using the calendar.

DIFFERENCES IN ETHNICITY

One of the most recently completed research projects using the instrument as presented in Table 5.1 (Study 4) is a Centers for Disease Control and Prevention funded prospective study of abuse during pregnancy (McFarlane et al., 1992). The sample was primarily the poor and approximately evenly divided into European American, African American, and Latino (mainly Mexican American). Of 329 women who were administered the Danger Assessment, 156 were classified as abused according to the Abuse Assessment Screen de-veloped in conjunction with the Nursing Research Consortium on Violence and Abuse (McFarlane et al., 1992; Parker & McFarlane, 1991). This operationalization of abuse uses the criterion of physical or sexual abuse within the last year. A body map and severity score are part of the Abuse Assessment Screen. In this study the European American women scored significantly higher than the other two groups on all measures of abuse, including the Danger Assessment, with the Latina women second highest, and the African American women lowest. In terms of prevalence of abuse, however, 19% of both European American and African American women reported abuse, and 14% of Latinas did so. More investigation is needed into the role of ethnicity in predicting homicide specific to battering situations.

FUTURE DEVELOPMENT OF THE DANGER ASSESSMENT

Development of the instrument continues. It is now being used in a major longitudinal study of women's responses to abuse that will yield further reliability and construct validity information. Future type predictive validity testing needs to be conducted before any formal prediction could be done by using this instrument. Two other studies have been launched to further test the Danger Assessment. The first is a post hoc predictive validity evaluation using police homicide files of women in Detroit. This effort is hampered by incomplete police information but will give important information on the items for which police data are kept. The second will estimate concurrent predictive validity in terms of the instrument's ability to discriminate correctly between battered women at high risk of homicide by other criteria (presenting at a hospital with serious injuries from abuse, or presenting to a shelter stating fear of being killed) and battered women in the community. The ideal predictive validity study would be to administer the instrument widely in a geographic locale and monitor the resultant homicides. As previously mentioned, the difficulty in predicting a relatively rare event such as a homicide necessitates a huge sample size in order to obtain significant results even if the instrument predicts accurately. Until this sort of study is done, however, cutoff scores, item weighting, or using the instrument for formal prediction is inadvisable.

Thus at this point the Danger Assessment instrument has sufficient statistical support for use in clinical settings for informal prediction. Battered women find discussing the instrument helpful in making decisions about what to do in their situations and how to monitor what is happening. Advocates and clinicians in many settings report finding the DA useful as an empowerment strategy for women and as helping them feel more comfortable in their clinical judgment. So far, the Danger Assessment remains the only instrument or list of risk factors with a program of instrument development research supporting its use, although the Straus instrument also has promise and no doubt will be developed further.

❏ **Conclusions**

It is not particularly useful to scare all battered women with dire predictions of homicide; neither is it ethically or legally responsible not to warn those in particular danger of their risk. The most difficult cases, of course, are those in which the degree of danger is not clearly apparent. It is also important to realize that some couples are mutually violent and will not present as the more usual battering pattern. These cases, too, can result in homicide (Campbell, 1992).

Should all cases in which abuse or mutual violence is detected be routinely assessed for homicide risk? Because abuse is such a serious risk factor for homicide between intimates, the answer is yes. Even in cases in which the risk is apparently low, knowledge of risk factors for homicide can be used later by the potential victim in decision making if the violence escalates, as it most often does. When dealing with the abused partner, she (or much less often, he) can be an active partner in determining the degree of danger and what she should do next. The clinician can present the instrument or list of danger signs to the victim and discuss how many are present and allow her to make her own decisions because there is a current absence of definitively established cutoff scores. Then the clinician and potential victim can discuss together possible actions. The risk is that the clinician becomes paternalistic

The abused partner can be an active participant in determining the degree of danger and what she should do next.

Table 5.2 Risk Factors Identified Across Majority of Experts

Access to/ownership of guns
Use of weapon in prior abusive incidents
Threats with weapon(s)
Threats to kill
Serious injury in prior abusive incidents
Threats of suicide
Drug or alcohol abuse
Forced sex of female partner
Obsessiveness/extreme jealousy/extreme dominance

---

and prescribes certain courses of action. At the same time, if the potential victim chooses not to take action to protect herself, the clinician may decide to call in the criminal justice system regardless, telling the potential victim of the decision and subsequent actions. The wife abuse shelter network also can be extremely helpful even if the woman decides not to actually go into the shelter.

As with most areas of violence, spousal homicide presents the dilemma of clinicians being caught between having both an ethical and a legal mandate to do accurate prediction without an unerring means of doing so. However, we have some information about risk factors, and both the clinical and the instrument lists currently in existence are remarkably similar. Table 5.2 presents a list of risk factors identified by the majority of the experts cited herein, including those on the Danger Assessment. All clinicians working with battered women and their abusers, whether in the mental health or physical health systems, the criminal justice system, or the shelter system, owe their clients a discussion of these homicide risk factors.

❏ **Note**

1. The Kuder Richardson formula is recommended to assess internal consistency for instruments such as the Danger Assessment that use nonweighted dichotomous responses (Knapp, 1991). When used with the Danger Assessment, however, it does not increase the reliability coefficient more than a hundredth of a point and therefore is not reported.

❏ References

Berk, R. A., Berk, S. F., Loseke, D. R., & Rauma, D. (1983). Mutual combat and other family violence myths. In D. Finkelhor, R. J. Gelles, G. T. Hotaling, & M. A. Straus (Eds.), *The dark side of families: Current family violence research* (pp. 197-212). Beverly Hills, CA: Sage.

Block, C. R. (1985). *Specification of patterns over time in Chicago homicide: Increases and decreases 1965-1981.* Chicago: Criminal Justice Information Authority.

Browne, A. (1987). *Battered women who kill.* New York: Free Press.

Campbell, J. C. (1981). Misogyny and homicide of women. *Advances in Nursing Science, 3*(2), 67-85.

Campbell, J. C. (1986). Assessment of risk of homicide for battered women. *Advances in Nursing Science, 8*(4), 36-51.

Campbell, J. C. (1992). "If I can't have you, no one can": Power and control in homicide of female partners. In J. Radford & D. Russell (Eds.), *Femicide: The politics of woman killing* (pp. 99-113). New York: Twayne.

Campbell, J. C., Miller, P., Cardwell, M., & Belknap, R. A. (1994). Relationship status of battered women over time. *Journal of Family Violence, 9,* 99-111.

Daly, M., & Wilson, M. (1988). *Homicide.* Hawthorne, NY: Aldine.

Department of Health and Human Services, Public Health Service (DHHS). (1990). *Healthy people 2000: National health promotion and disease prevention objectives.* Washington, DC: Government Printing Office.

Fagan, J. A., Stewart, D. K., & Hansen, K. V. (1983). Violent men or violent husbands? Background factors and situational correlates. In D. Finkelhor, R. J. Gelles, G. T. Hotaling, & M. A. Straus (Eds.), *The dark side of families: Current family violence research* (pp. 49-68). Beverly Hills, CA: Sage.

Farley, R. (1986). Homicide trends in the United States. In D. F. Hawkins (Ed.), *Homicide among black Americans* (pp. 13-27). New York: University Press of America.

Ferraro, K. J., & Johnson, J. M. (1983). How women experience battering: The process of victimization. *Social Problems, 30,* 325-339.

Hart, B. (1988). Beyond the "duty to warn": A therapist's "duty to protect" battered women and children. In K. Yllö & M. Bograd (Eds.), *Feminist perspectives on wife abuse* (pp. 234-248). Newbury Park, CA: Sage.

Hudson, W., & McIntosh, S. (1981). The index of spouse abuse. *Journal of Marriage and the Family, 43*(4), 873-888.

Humphrey, J. A., Hudson, R. P., & Cosgrove, S. (1981). Women who are murdered: An analysis of 912 consecutive victims. *OMEGA, 12*(3), 281-288.

Jurik, N. C., & Winn, R. (1990). Gender and homicide: A comparison of men and women who kill. *Violence and Victims, 5,* 227-242.

Knapp, T. R. (1991). Focus on psychometrics—coefficient alpha: Conceptualizations and anomalies. *Research in Nursing and Health, 14,* 457-460.

Mann, C. R. (1990). Black female homicide in the United States. *Journal of Interpersonal Violence, 5,* 176-201.

McFarlane, J., Parker, B., Soeken, K., & Bullock, L. (1992). Assessing for abuse during pregnancy: Severity and frequency of injuries and associated entry into prenatal care. *Journal of the American Medical Association, 267,* 3176-3178.

Mercy, J. A., & Saltzman, L. E. (1989). Fatal violence among spouses in the United States, 1976-85. *American Journal of Public Health, 79,* 595-599.

Miller, M., & Morris, N. (1988). Predictions of dangerousness: An argument for limited use. *Violence and Victims, 3*(4), 263-283.

Okun, L. E. (1986). *Woman abuse: Facts replacing myths.* Albany: State University of New York Press.

Parker, B., & McFarlane, J. (1991). Identifying and helping battered pregnant women. *Maternal Child Nursing, 16*(3), 161-164.

Small, L. B. (1985). Psychotherapists' duty to warn: Ten years after *Tarasoff. Golden Gate University Law Review, 15*(2), 271-300.

Sonkin, D. J., Martin, D., & Walker, L. E. (1985). *The male batterer: A treatment approach.* New York: Springer.

Straus, M. A., & Gelles, R. J. (1990). *Physical violence in American families: Risk factors and adaptions to violence in 8,145 families.* New Brunswick, NJ: Transaction Books.

Straus, M. J. (1991, November). *Severity and chronicity of domestic assault: Measurement implications for criminal justice intervention.* Paper presented at the Annual American Society of Criminology Conference, San Francisco.

Stuart, E. P., & Campbell, J. C. (1989). Assessment of patterns of dangerousness with battered women. *Issues in Mental Health Nursing, 10,* 245-260.

Wallace, A. (1986). A typology of homicide. In A. Wallace (Ed.), *Homicide: The social reality* (pp. 83-109). New South Wales: Bureau of Crime Statistics and Research.

Wilbanks, W. (1986). Criminal homicide offenders in the U.S.: Black vs. white. In D. F. Hawkins (Ed.), *Homicide among black Americans* (pp. 43-55). New York: University Press of America.

Wilson, M. (1991, November). *Problems in defining marital-like relationships.* Paper presented at the meetings of the American Society of Criminology, San Francisco.

6

Predicting Sexual Offenses

Vernon L. Quinsey
Martin L. Lalumière
Marnie E. Rice
Grant T. Harris

❏ Introduction

Forensic clinicians are asked frequently to appraise the degree of risk that a sex offender poses to the community. These judgments, whether based on actuarial information, clinical intuition, or a combination of these, often have an important impact on the liberty of the individual and the amount of risk of new victimization to which

AUTHORS' NOTE: The review portion of this chapter borrows, in part, from Quinsey (1984, 1986) and Quinsey and Lalumière (in press). Preparation of this chapter was supported by a contract between the first author and the Kingston Psychiatric Hospital and by a Fellowship from the Social Sciences and Humanities Research Council of Canada accorded to the second author. The follow-up study was supported by Ontario Ministry of Health Research Grant 01430 to the third and fourth authors.

the community is exposed. In addition to the substantive issues pertaining to the accuracy of these judgments is a set of legal and professional regulations that forms the context within which appraisals of dangerousness must be made.

Most jurisdictions have legal statutes that govern dispositional decisions concerning sex offenders. Among the most controversial of these are "criminal sexual psychopath" or "dangerous sexual offender" statutes that aim to incapacitate dangerous offenders through preventive detention (for reviews of these issues see Greenland, 1984; Pallone, 1990; Wormith & Ruhl, 1986). These statutes often specify legal criteria for determining whether a convicted offender or a person found not criminally responsible for an offense because of mental disorder is to be detained in custody and whether that detention is to be for an indeterminate or determinate duration.

Although criminal and mental health laws specify the criteria by which judicial or quasi-judicial bodies are to make decisions about sex offenders, legislative language must in some way be related to the empirical literature on the prediction of recidivism if these laws are likely to achieve their social purpose. This chapter focuses on the substantive, as opposed to the legal, issues involved in prediction. Readers should be aware, however, that once an appraisal of risk has been made, it must be related to a jurisdiction's particular legal and policy context to be useful to persons making dispositional decisions.

The most important aspect of the policy context within which an assessment is conducted concerns what negative outcomes of release or relaxation of supervision are to be predicted. We could be concerned about a psychiatric relapse, criminal recidivism of any kind, violent recidivism, and/or sexual recidivism. The distinction among these is important because their likelihood for any given offender may be very different. If we were to be concerned with minor offenses or reinstitutionalization, for example, we would be much more likely to conclude that an offender was high risk than if we were to be concerned only with more serious (and much rarer) phenomena. In this chapter we deal primarily with appraising the risk of new violent or sex offenses among men who are known to have committed at least one sex offense in the past.

❑ Follow-Up Studies

In this section follow-up studies of convicted sex offenders are reviewed in an attempt to estimate the proportion of offenders who are likely to recidivate; this proportion is known as the *base rate.* Base rates have profound effects on the accuracy that can be achieved in prediction (e.g., see Quinsey, 1980). Put simply, if the base rate of recidivism for a given population is extremely low, then the best prediction for any offender in that group is that he or she will not reoffend and that it is useless to attempt to do better by assessing individual cases. The converse holds for a population with an extremely high base rate (the best prediction is that everyone will reoffend).

Recidivism rates can be expected to vary according to the offense history and demographic characteristics of the population studied. In addition to the characteristics of the sample studied, methodological factors affect recidivism rates across studies. These include the definition of recidivism and way it is measured (self-reported reoffending, arrests, charges, or convictions) and the length of the follow-up (including the amount of opportunity to reoffend).

One of the most crucial pieces of information obtained from follow-up studies concerns offender and situational variables related to recidivism. Variables that cannot be changed through active intervention, such as offense history, age, and demographic characteristics, are called *static predictors,* whereas variables that are changeable, such as procriminal attitudes or quality of supervision, are termed *dynamic predictors.* Static predictors can be used to determine the degree of risk that an offender presents. Dynamic predictors, however, are the focus of treatment and supervision because they involve issues about which something can be done and can, at least in principle, modify an offender's level of risk. Unfortunately few sex offender follow-up studies have attempted to identify variables that predict recidivism, and even fewer have attempted to identify dynamic predictors. Static predictors thus have much greater empirical support for making predictions.

A number of considerations are of concern in interpreting the results of a particular follow-up study. The ideal study would consist of a long follow-up period (at least 5 years) of one or more homogeneous groups of sex offenders for whom descriptions of offenses resulting in rearrests and reconvictions are available for both sexual and nonsexual offenses. Recidivism rates would be adjusted for opportunity to reoffend. Recidivists and nonrecidivists would be compared on a number of static and theoretically relevant dynamic predictors in order to determine risk status and targets for intervention.

Follow-up studies are reviewed below in light of these considerations. Studies of rapists are presented first, followed by studies of child molesters. Because of changes in sex offender legislation and societal responses to sexual crimes over time, these studies are presented in chronological order of the cohort studied. For the purpose of exposition we have restricted our survey to studies that reported sexual reoffense data for rapists and/or child molesters separately. We focus on these sex offenders because they are among the most serious and because most of the prediction literature deals with them. Studies that have reported data for undifferentiated sex offenders—that is, groups comprised of rapists, child molesters, exhibitionists, and so on—are not included here (e.g., see Christiansen, Elers-Nielsen, Le Maire, & Sturup, 1965; Gray & Mohr, 1965; Hall & Proctor, 1987; see Quinsey, 1984, 1986, for reviews). The few studies that have focused primarily on treatment outcome have been reviewed elsewhere (e.g., Marshall & Barbaree, 1990; Quinsey, Harris, Rice, & Lalumière, in press). The interested reader is also invited to consult Furby, Weinrott, and Blackshaw (1989) for more information on recidivism rates of other types of sex offenders.

FOLLOW-UP STUDIES OF RAPISTS

Soothill, Jack, and Gibbens (1976) conducted a 22 year follow-up of 86 offenders convicted of rape in 1951 in England or Wales; 30% of the sample had no prior convictions for any offense, and 16% had prior convictions for sexual offenses; 6% had a subsequent conviction for rape, 15% for a sexual offense of any kind, 20% for a violent offense against the person (34% if robbery was included), and 49% were convicted for any offense. Unfortunately the time at risk was not reported. Interestingly, the six rapes (committed by five offenders) occurred over a relatively long period—that is, as long as 18 years after the beginning of the follow-up. In contrast, 55% of all offenses occurred in the first 7 years.

The Cambridge study examined a large number of sex offenses committed in England during 1951 (Radzinowicz, 1957). The sexual reconviction rate of 40 men convicted of a sex offense against women was 10% in a 4-year follow-up.

As part of a large follow-up study of sex offenders treated and released from the Atascadero maximum security psychiatric institution in California, Frisbie and Dondis (1965) followed 70 men who had committed sexual acts on females 18 years of age or older accompanied by threat or force. The cumulative 5-year sexual reconviction rate was 36%.

Romero and Williams (1985) conducted a 10-year follow-up of 144 sexual assaulters placed on probation in Philadelphia between 1966 and 1969. Sexual assaulters were offenders against a female victim of 13 years of age or older or of a female victim of 11 or 12 years old when the offender was younger than 21; 10% were rearrested at least once for a sexual offense, and 63% were rearrested for any offense. These numbers are likely to underestimate actual reoffense rates because the arrest records were only available for offenders after age 18, only arrests in the Philadelphia area were recorded, and some offenders were not at risk to recidivate.

Grunfeld and Noreik (1986) conducted a follow-up averaging 12 years in duration of 83 first offenders who had received a legal sanction for rape between 1970 and 1974 (about half of all rapists for that period of time in Norway). The reconviction rates were 21% for "felonies against public morals" (any sex offense) and 10% for rape. The average time between the release from prison and the first sexual reoffense was 14 months (ranging from 6 to 97); 9% had had prior sanctions for crimes of violence, and 45% for crimes of profit; 16% and 40% were reconvicted for crimes of violence and crimes of profit, respectively, during the follow-up period.

Most rapes occurred within the first year of the follow-up.

As part of a large sample of sex offenders, Sturgeon and Taylor (1980) followed 57 mentally disordered rapists treated and discharged from Atascadero State Hospital, California, in 1973. *Rape* was defined as an attempt "or actual genital or oral-genital contact with a non-consanguine female victim, 14 years of age or older, when force, assault or direct threat of such were involved in the contact or attempted contact" (p. 35); 38% had a prior conviction for sexual crimes, 16% for nonsexual crimes against persons, and 56% for crimes against property. Within a 5-year period, 19% of these rapists were reconvicted for sexual crimes, 14% for nonsexual crimes against persons, and less than 2% for crimes against property. Most rapes occurred within the first year of the follow-up.

Sturgeon and Taylor also reported data from a sample of 68 rapists convicted of a sexual crime but not found to be mentally disordered sex offenders. These subjects were paroled from prison from 1973 and followed for 5 years. Prior and subsequent convictions were, respectively, 21% and 28% for sexual crimes, 35% and 16% for nonsexual crimes against persons, and 68% and 28% for crimes against property.

Finally, Rice, Harris, and Quinsey (1990) studied 54 sex offenders who had sexually assaulted (or attempted to sexually assault) a female of 14 years of age or older. All subjects were released before 1983 and were followed for an average of 4 years; 28% had a subsequent conviction for sexual offenses, 43% had a subsequent arrest or conviction for violent offenses (including sex offenses), and 59% had a subsequent arrest or conviction for any offense or had been returned to maximum security for any reason. Sexual recidivists, compared with nonrecidivists, had more serious sexual offense histories, higher psychopathy scores, and more phallometrically measured sexual interest in nonsexual violence against women. Noteworthily, psychopathy and phallometric scores could predict sexual reconvictions as well as any combinations of other variables, including offense history variables. On the basis of these two variables, 77% of rapists were correctly classified as sexual recidivists or nonrecidivists.

Summary of Follow-Up Studies of Rapists

The follow-up studies of convicted rapists ($N = 458$) showed a weighted[1] average *sexual* (any sexual offense) *reconviction* rate of 22.8% (range of 10% to 36%). Sample recidivism values (for the seven independent samples reporting reconviction rates) significantly differed from one another ($\chi^2(6) = 16.11, p < .05$; test of homogeneity, Fleiss, 1973), implying that some study and/or sample characteristics, such as length of follow-up, cause variation in recidivism rates. This statistically significant variation in recidivism rates means that the average recidivism rate reported above is a rather uninformative estimate of the reconviction rate of rapists. Unfortunately the large number of study/sample characteristics that could have produced the observed variability among sample recidivism rates compared to the small number of studies available prevents further analysis. The average base rate obtained, however, supports the idea that assessment of risk among rapists can be fruitful.

As would be expected from the relation between previous sexual offense history and recidivism, the proportion of rapists who had previous sexual convictions was relatively similar to the proportion of rapists who incurred sexual reconvictions during the follow-up period in most of the studies. Rates of reoffending decreased with the seriousness of the index offense (e.g., from nonviolent nonsexual to violent sexual). Finally, two theoretically and clinically relevant predictors—psychopathy and phallometric scores—were found in a recent study to accurately predict sexual reconviction. These two variables performed as well as a combination of a large number of historical variables.

FOLLOW-UP STUDIES OF CHILD MOLESTERS

In the Cambridge study, Radzinowicz (1957) studied 1,985 sex offenders before the courts. The offenders were followed up for a 4-year period subsequent to their conviction or release from prison. Of the 1,985 offenders, 83% had never been convicted for a sexual offense previously; however, about one fourth admitted to having committed previous sexual offenses. The proportion of offenders who had had previous convictions was higher for men offending against boys than girls.

In this sample, 20% were reconvicted of a sexual offense. Of the heterosexual child molesters, 13% were reconvicted; the comparable figure for homosexual child molesters was 27%. New sexual offenses usually involved the same type of victim. Men who were already sexual recidivists before the follow-up began were more likely to reoffend.

Fitch (1962) studied 139 men convicted of sex crimes against children (aged less than 16 years) and sent to a British prison between 1951 and 1956—21% of the 77 heterosexual offenders had had at least one prior conviction for sexual offending; the comparable value for the 62 homosexual offenders was 48%. Subsequent reconvictions were recorded for the period between the release of the offenders and 1960 (a range of 1 to 9 years); 13% of heterosexual offenders and 40% of homosexual offenders were reconvicted for sexual offenses; 8% of heterosexual *incest* offenders and 16% of heterosexual nonincest offenders were reconvicted of a new sexual offense. The 35 sexual recidivists were more likely to be homosexual, had more previous convictions for sexual offenses, were younger at conviction for the first sexual offense, and were more likely to be single than the remainder of the sample. Age at the time of the offense, number of previous nonsexual convictions, intelligence, and employment status did not differentiate the two groups.

In a more recent English study, Gibbens, Soothill, and Way (1981) followed 48 men charged in 1951 with unlawful sexual intercourse with an unrelated female under 13 years of age, as well as a similar sample of 62 men charged in 1961; 60% had had no previous serious offenses, and 11% had been convicted previously for sex crimes. Many of the previous offenses were against property. In the 24-year follow-up period for the 1951 group, 46% were reconvicted and 19% were convicted for a new sexual offense against girls under age 13. These calculations were adjusted for opportunity to reoffend.

In the 1961 group the comparable figures for the 15-year follow-up were 35% and 5%. Gibbens et al. observed that these offenders continued to be convicted of new sexual offenses for very long periods after their index offense and concluded that sex crimes against young children do not show the fast drop in frequency with age that is characteristic of property offenses.

In a separate study Gibbens, Soothill, and Way (1978) followed 114 father-daughter incest offenders for approximately 10 years starting in 1965; 13% had prior sexual offenses, and 4% had prior violent offenses; 4% had subsequent convictions for sexual offenses, and 2% for violent offenses.

Frisbie and Dondis (1965) studied "sexual psychopaths" who had been treated in a maximum security psychiatric institution in California and discharged to the court as improved. Based on the relation of the victim to the offender and victim gender, the sample consisted of 1,035 heterosexual, 428 homosexual, and 49 bisexual child molesters. In the heterosexual sample were 318 cases of father-daughter incest or father-stepdaughter "incest." The victims in both kinds of incest cases tended to be older (8 to 17 years of age) than the unrelated victims, who were usually under age 11.

Recidivists tended to be younger and were more frequently previously diagnosed as sociopathic.

The incest offenders had a cumulative 6-year sexual recidivism rate of 10%, the heterosexual offenders against children less than 13 years of age had a recidivism rate of 22%, and the recidivism rate for homosexual child molesters was 35%. Most reoffenders maintained the gender of the victim involved in the index offense. The recidivism rate of the bisexual offenders was similar to that of the heterosexual offenders. Recidivists tended to be younger and were more frequently previously diagnosed as sociopathic.

In a sequel to the Frisbie and Dondis study, Frisbie (1969) conducted a follow-up of 887 men 18 years of age or older convicted of a sexual offense involving bodily contact with a minor under age 18; 75% of the offenders were heterosexual. An effort was made to interview offenders whose victims were less than 14 years of age and offenders who were already sexual recidivists. Of the 617 offenders who were released, 15% were convicted of a new sexual offense within 3.5 years. Frisbie concluded on the basis of the follow-up interviews that economic stress, overcrowding and lack of privacy, unsatisfactory familial relationships, difficulties in occupational or social situations, health problems, and aging were unrelated to recidivism. Instead the following variables were statistically related to recidivism: alcohol abuse, unorthodox ethical values, problems in establishing meaningful relationships with adult females, and the desire for physically immature females as sexual objects.

Sturgeon and Taylor (1980), as part of their extensive study of a large sample of sex offenders, also report follow-up data from homosexual ($n = 55$) and heterosexual ($n = 91$) pedophiles and incest offenders ($n = 57$). Pedophiles were offenders convicted of "any sexual offense whose non-consanguine victim is less than 14 years of age; or any offense on a non-consanguine victim, ages 14 through 17, when assault, force or threat of force were not direct factors in sexual contact or attempted contact; or a sexual offense involving multiple victims, at least one of whom was less than 14 years of age and non-consanguine" (p. 35). Incest offenders were convicted with any sexual offense whose victim was a consanguine relative. Subjects were mentally disordered sex offenders and treated as part of the Atascadero program. The authors also included data from subjects paroled from prison from 1973 (16 homosexual and 28 heterosexual pedophiles, and 10 incest offenders). Subjects were followed for 5 years.

Homosexual pedophiles had the highest rate of prior convictions for sexual crimes (53%, 69% for the prison cohort), compared with heterosexual pedophiles (43%, 36%) and incest offenders (11%, 20%). Homosexual pedophiles also had the highest rate of prior convictions for nonsexual crimes against persons (22%, 13%), compared with heterosexual (9%, 7%) and incest offenders (2%, 9%). Prior convictions for crimes against property were higher than 45% for all groups.

The reconviction rate for sexual crimes was also higher for homosexual pedophiles (30%, 38% for the prison sample), compared with heterosexual pedophiles (25%, 18%) and incest offenders (6%, 25%). Reconviction rates for nonsexual crimes against persons followed the same pattern and varied from 0% (incest offenders, prison cohort) to 26% (homosexual pedophiles, patient cohort). Reconviction rates for crimes against property varied between 10% (incest offenders, prison cohort) and 28% (homosexual pedophiles, prison cohort). Contrary to the rapist samples reported above, reoffenses seemed to be distributed evenly in the first 3 years of the follow-up.

Grunfeld and Noreik (1986) followed 279 child molesters who had received, between 1970 and 1974, a legal sanction for felonies under the category "sexual abuse of a minor" (defined as indecent relations with a child below the age of 16). This sample comprised about half of all child molesters convicted during that period in Norway. Subjects were followed for an average of 12 years (range 9 to 14 years); 10% received a subsequent legal sanction for "felonies against public morals" (any sex offense), and 7% offended against children again. The average time between release from prison and the first sexual reoffense was 46 months (range 3 to 100); 4% had had prior sanctions for crimes of violence and 30% for crimes of profit; 10% and 24% were convicted for a crime of violence and crimes of profit, respectively, during the follow-up period.

In a recent study Barbaree and Marshall (1988) followed 35 extrafamilial sex offenders against victims under age 16 (21 against female victims, and 14 against male victims). Recidivism data were based on both official and unofficial reports (the latter showing 2.7 times the rate of reoffending). From both kinds of reports, 43% reoffended sexually during a 4-year follow-up period ranging from 1 to 9 years. No difference was found between the recidivism rates of heterosexual and homosexual offenders. The authors calculated three orthogonal factors from a large pool of variables collected from a larger sample of child molesters ($n = 126$). The three factors were Sexual Deviance (a deviance index derived from phallometric assessment, use of force, intercourse, and number of victims), Social Status (intelligence quotient, socioeconomic status), and Offender Age (age of offender, age of victim).

Taken together, the factors explained 20% of the variance in the recidivism of the 35 offenders. Sexual Deviance explained 19% of the total variance. Variables loading on the Sexual Deviance factor yielded 71% correct classification (42% relative improvement over chance). The following individual variables were positively associated with recidivism: use of force during the offense, number of previous victims, and sexual deviance quotient.

In another recent study Rice, Quinsey, and Harris (1991) followed 136 extrafamilial child molesters (defined as men who had had physical sexual contact with a girl under age 14 when at least 5 years older than the victim, or with a boy under age 16 when at least 5 years older than the victim). Subjects were released before 1983 and followed for an average of 6.3 years; 31% had a subsequent conviction for a sexual offense; 43% had a subsequent violent arrest (violent offenses were defined to include sexual offenses), and 56% failed for any reason. Sexual recidivists, compared with nonrecidivists, were less likely to have been married, more likely to have been diagnosed as personality disordered, had a more serious sexual offense history, and showed more deviant phallometrically measured sexual preferences. A discriminant function using these and other variables was able to classify correctly 80% of sexual recidivists and nonrecidivists.

Summary of Follow-Up Studies of Child Molesters

The weighted average *sexual reconviction* rates (any sexual offense) for the 17 independent samples (N = 4,483) of child molesters was 20.4% (range of 4% to 38%). Study recidivism values differed significantly from one another ($\chi^2(16) = 166.87, p < .001$), suggesting the presence of study and/or sample characteristics specifically related to recidivism.

As was the case for rapists, this weighted average is not a very informative estimate of the reconviction rate of child molesters. Some study and sample characteristics, such as gender and relation to the child victims, produce variations in recidivism rates. Other relevant characteristics might very well include methodological factors such as the definition of the sample (age of the offenders' child victims vary across studies from less than 13 years to less than 18 years) and the length of follow-up periods. Differences in legislation and in police, prosecutor, and victim behavior over time and place also create artificial variations in recidivism rates across studies.

We analyzed the studies according to whether the offenders contacted female victims (7 samples), male victims (4 samples), or were exclusively incestuous (4 samples) when the information available was adequate. The weighted average *sexual reconviction* rates for heterosexual samples (excluding samples of exclusive incest offenders) was 18.3% (N = 1,167). The comparable value for samples of homosexual child molesters (again excluding samples of exclusive incest offenders) was 35.2% (N = 561). Samples of exclusive incest offenders showed an average of 8.5% (N = 499). The heterosexual child molester samples ($\chi^2(6) = 37.79, p < .001$) and the incest offender samples ($\chi^2(3) = 7.87, p < .05$) were heterogeneous. This was not the case for the homosexual samples ($\chi^2(3) = 1.34$, n.s.). Overall, these averages give support to the idea that homosexual offenders have a higher rate of sexual recidivism than heterosexual offenders and that extrafamilial offenders have a higher rate of sexual recidivism than incest offenders. (It should be pointed out that some heterosexual samples included in these calculations contained some incest offenders.) Studies comparing these three types of offenders within the same setting have arrived at similar conclusions (e.g., Fitch, 1962; Frisbie & Dondis, 1965; Hanson, Steffy, & Gauthier, 1993; Sturgeon & Taylor, 1980; but see Barbaree & Marshall, 1988).

It is worth noting that the well-accepted notion that rapists' offense histories and subsequent reoffending include more nonsexual violent offenses, compared with child molesters (e.g., Christiansen et al., 1965; Grunfeld & Noreik, 1986; Hall & Proctor, 1987; Romero & Williams, 1985) is not invariably true. On the one hand, child molesters referred to maximum security psychiatric institutions for assessment or treatment appear to be relatively versatile offenders, much like rapists. Incest offenders, on the other hand, show very low rates of nonsexual violent offending across studies.

CONCLUSIONS FROM THE FOLLOW-UP LITERATURE

One must remember in interpreting follow-up data that reports of convictions underestimate the amount of reoffending that actually occurred. Small numbers of sexual assaulters commit large numbers of offenses for which they are seldom charged. For example, Abel et al. (1987) collected, using Certificates of Confidentiality from the U.S. Department of Health, Education, and Welfare, self-reports of previous offenses from 561 nonincarcerated sex offenders. The 244 offenders who had molested female children reported an average of 19 victims (median = 1.3); men who had molested male children averaged 150 victims (median = 4.4).

From the follow-up studies of sex offenders reviewed above, it can be seen that, with the exception of heterosexual incest offenders, the base rate of sexual recidivism is high enough to make individual assessments of dangerousness potentially fruitful. Although absolute rates of recidivism show considerable variability across samples, conclusions about relative recidivism rates can be drawn more easily. Among child molesters, those whose victims are male have the highest recidivism rates; those with unrelated females, lower rates; and heterosexual incest offenders, the lowest rates. Evidence also suggests that laboratory-measured (but not self-reported) deviant sexual interest is related to recidivism. The rate of sexual recidivism among child molesters (especially heterosexual offenders) substantially overlaps that of rapists, and the likelihood of subsequent sexual recidivism is related to the number of prior sexual offenses in both groups of offenders. Similarly the prediction literature on undifferentiated or mixed groups of sex offenders has shown consistently that past criminality is associated with higher probability of reoffending (e.g., Christiansen et al., 1965; Correctional Services of Canada, 1991).

In addition to the reasonably high base rate of sexual recidivism among sex offenders, the observation that a variety of offender characteristics are reliably related to the probability of recidivism strongly supports attempts to make individual assessments of risk. In the next section we describe an empirical strategy in assessing risk by using theoretically and clinically relevant variables.

❏ A Risk Prediction Instrument for Rapists and Child Molesters

As described above, laboratory-measured deviant sexual interest is related to sexual recidivism. It has been known for some time from offender self-reports and from phallometric assessments that sexual preferences and fantasies play an important role in motivating sex offenses of various kinds. This evidence appears most compelling for extrafamilial child molestation and rape (e.g., Freund & Blanchard, 1989; Lalumière & Quinsey, 1993, 1994; MacCulloch, Snowden, Wood, & Mills, 1983; Quinsey & Chaplin, 1988a; Quinsey, Chaplin, & Upfold, 1984). In particular, the ability of phallometric assessments of age and gender preferences to discriminate extrafamilial child molesters from nonsex offenders has not been seriously questioned. This discriminative ability exists not only because inappropriate sexual age preferences are detectable in a substantial proportion of child molesters but also because they are very seldom detected among non-child molesters (Freund & Blanchard, 1989). Although more controversial, a considerable body of evidence now suggests that phallometric assessments of preference for various consenting and nonconsenting sexual and violent activities directed toward adults of the preferred gender can discriminate rapists from nonrapists (Harris, Rice, Quinsey, Chaplin, & Earls, 1992; Lalumière & Quinsey, 1993, 1994). The sensitivity of phallometric measures of sexual preference for nonconsensual sexual interactions obtained with rapists are similar to values obtained in assessments of sexual age preferences among child molesters (Lalumière & Quinsey, 1993).

It is clear, however, from the research reviewed above and from other studies, that there is more to sexual offending and reoffending than inappropriate sexual preferences. As reviewed above, variables related to criminal history (including sexual offense history), victim choice (including age, gender, and relationship of the victim), as well as offender variables such as age and marital status, have been shown to be related to recidivism.

> *There is more to sexual offending and reoffending than inappropriate sexual preferences.*

Another factor that may be involved, although it has seldom been investigated, is psychopathy. *Psychopaths* are persons who exhibit characteristics such as impulsivity, lack of empathy, parasitic lifestyle, and sexual promiscuity (Hare, 1991). Whereas some nonpsychopathic men may have deviant sexual interests but inhibit their expression for a variety of reasons, psychopathic men may obtain sexual gratification opportunistically regardless of whether it involves their preferred mode of sexual activity or whether it is legal.

Hare (1991) developed a rating scale of psychopathy, the Psychopathy Checklist (PCL-R), that has high interrater reliability and is strongly related to a varied criminal history, including the commission of sexual and violent crimes (e.g., Hare & McPherson, 1984). Inmates who score high on the PCL-R are prone to exhibit instrumental, as opposed to angry, aggression, use weapons, and select victims who are unknown to them (Serin, 1991; Williamson, Hare, & Wong, 1987). Harris, Rice, and Cormier (1991) found that psychopathy was an excellent predictor of violent recidivism in a maximum security psychiatric sample, and Rice et al. (1990) found that PCL-R score was related to recidivism in a sample of rapists.

We present in this section a synopsis of a recent effort to develop a risk prediction instrument that includes theoretically and clinically relevant variables. This instrument was constructed on a mixed sample of 178 rapists and child molesters released from a maximum security psychiatric facility. A large part of this sample was reported on in Rice et al. (1990) and Rice et al. (1991). A detailed description of the subjects, method, and analyses leading to the results summarized below is presented in Quinsey et al. (in press).

RECIDIVISM

Among the 178 rapists and child molesters, 49 (27.5%) subsequently were convicted of a new sexual offense; 72 (40.4%) were arrested, convicted, or returned to the institution for a violent offense against persons or a sexual offense; and 99 (55.6%) were arrested. The group averaged approximately 50 months of opportunity to reoffend during the follow-up period. Sexual recidivists were significantly differentiated by their previous record of sexual offenses, previous general criminal history, marital status, Psychopathy Checklist score, and phallometric deviance index.

Survival functions were calculated for sexual reconvictions for the three groups of offenders: rapists ($n = 28$), child molesters ($n = 124$, including 13 incest offenders), and 26 mixed offenders. Survival functions represent the proportion of the sample remaining at risk in a given year of follow-up time. A straight horizontal curve would indicate that no subject recidivated throughout the follow-up period. A decelerating downward curve would indicate that most failures occurred at the beginning of the follow-up period.

The survival curves for all subjects were not horizontal and did not decelerate over time; that is, there was no evidence of "burn out," and risk was as great in the 7th year, for example, as it was in the first. Rapists represented considerably greater risk than child molesters throughout the follow-up period in that a smaller proportion of the rapist sample remained at risk at each year of the follow-up period.

RISK PREDICTION

Table 6.1 shows the correlation between each of the predictor variables and sexual reconviction. Elsewhere (Quinsey et al., in press) we have presented the results of a multiple regression analysis in which we predicted sexual reconviction from a linear combination of the variables shown in Table 6.1. However, multiple regression results are known to exhibit considerable shrinkage (in variance accounted for) on cross-validation (on a new sample of individuals) because regression coefficients are computed so as to maximize fit

Table 6.1 Significant Correlation ($p < .05$) Between Study Variables and Sexual Reconviction

Variables	r	
Prior violent convictions	.22	***
Prior convictions for other offenses	.14	*
Prior convictions for sex offenses	.26	***
Never married	.22	**
Previous admissions to corrections	.20	**
Previous admissions to Oak Ridge	.18	**
Previous female victim	.17	**
Previous male victim	.20	**
Previous child victim	.22	**
Previous adult victim	.13	*
Psychopathy Checklist	.18	**
Deviance Index[a]	−.21	**
Number of male victims	.17	*

a. A negative index indicates a more deviant profile.
* $p < .05$; ** $p < .01$; *** $p < .001$. One-tailed tests.

between predictors and the outcome variable on the particular sample studied. To reduce the amount of shrinkage obtained on cross-validation, we employed the Nuffield (1982) method to construct a recidivism prediction instrument.

In the Nuffield method, predictor variables are selected according to their univariate relationships with the outcome variable. In the prediction equation, each variable is assigned a positive or negative integer value (the weight) that depends both on the subject's score on that variable and on the overall magnitude of the relationship between that predictor variable and the outcome. For each category or value of each predictor for which the recidivism differed by 5% from the average rate, a weight of plus or minus one is assigned; for differences of plus or minus 10%, a weight of plus or minus two is assigned, and so on. This is done for each predictor, and the weights then are summed to determine each subject's score. This method yielded in this sample a correlation of .45 between subjects' scores and sexual reconviction.

Figure 6.1 illustrates the performance of the Nuffield method using all variables presented in Table 6.1. The Nuffield method yielded 77% correct decisions in classifying sexual recidivist and nonrecidivist and

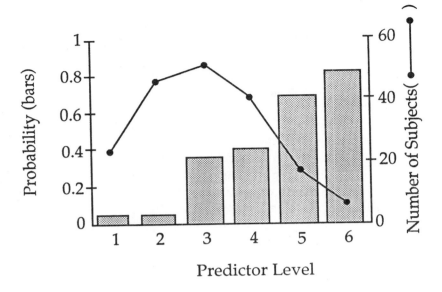

Figure 6.1. Actuarial Results for Sexual Reconviction Using the Nuffield Method

a relative improvement over chance of 44% ($\chi^2(1) = 25.13, p < .0001$) when the selection ratio was set approximately equal to the base rate. Figure 6.1 shows that the probability of reoffending increases monotonically as a function of the predictor level (or level of risk). Also the number of individuals predicted by the Nuffield method to commit a new offense was smaller at the extremes of the predictor level.

CONCLUSIONS AND DISCUSSION

The statistical instrument presented here shows that sexual recidivism was well predicted by previous criminal history, psychopathy ratings, and phallometric assessment data. More importantly, the Nuffield method yielded a risk score that was linearly related to sexual recidivism. This linear relationship allows a systematic approach to deciding about the required intensity of treatment and supervision, in addition to simply making a binary decision of whether to place or hold an offender in an institution. Supervision and treatment are administered most profitably to higher risk cases (Andrews et al., 1990). To the extent that decisions involve differential treatment and supervision, as opposed to incarceration, the cost of false positive errors (those persons incorrectly classified as dangerous) can be reduced (Quinsey & Walker, 1992).

This strategy is not that of taking an actuarial estimate as an additional piece of information to combine with a clinical appraisal of dangerousness, but rather to anchor clinical judgment by having the clinician start with an actuarial estimate of risk and then to alter it by examining dynamic variables such as treatment outcome and intensity and quality of supervision. Anchoring clinical judgments is not a new idea; it forms the basis of the method for structuring discretion in parole and sentencing (Gottfredson, Wilkins, & Hoffman, 1978). This strategy is recommended because of the well-known inadequacy of unaided clinical predictions, particularly those involving violent or sexual offending (e.g., Quinsey & Ambtman, 1979; Quinsey & Maguire, 1986). Part of the inaccuracy of clinical judgment is due to the insensitivity of clinicians to base rate information, an issue directly dealt with by actuarial estimates.

From the literature review presented earlier, it is clear that particular samples of sex offenders vary widely in their recidivism rates. Such variations in the base rate have profound effects on predictive accuracy. Therefore the actuarial scheme presented here (and described in complete detail in Quinsey, Harris, & Rice, in press) cannot be used to estimate specific recidivism probabilities for offender samples with characteristics different from the those of the sample used to construct the scale. However, it is likely (and empirically testable) that our actuarial scale would be successful in *ranking* child molesters and rapists from samples with different characteristics according to their level of risk.

❏ **Future Directions**

The prediction results presented in this chapter encourage the development of actuarial instruments for the prediction of sexual recidivism in any situation in which appreciable numbers of high-risk sex offenders are assessed. Predictive accuracy can be enhanced by including sex offense history, psychopathy, and phallometrically measured sexual preferences as predictors. Policies then can be developed that relate scores on the actuarial instrument to supervisory and treatment decisions.

Although the predictive results are quite good, future research can improve the accuracy of actuarial assessment by improving any of the predictors involved. Phallometric assessment data are a good case in point. Although these data are quite specific, their sensitivity could be improved considerably. Among the most obvious ways of improving sensitivity is by developing methods to detect or eliminate faking (e.g., Lalumière & Earls, 1992; Quinsey & Chaplin, 1988b).

The most important need at present is the identification and evaluation of dynamic predictors. These are of several kinds. First are situational predictors, including such things as gaining or losing employment. Second are changes in attitude or mood (which may or may not be related to identifiable situational phenomena). Third are treatment-induced changes, such as skill acquisition. It is highly likely that the most relevant dynamic predictors will involve criminogenic needs (the antecedents of sexual offending) or variables related to the opportunity to commit further offenses, such as compliance with supervision. The ultimate result of research on dynamic factors is the ability to specify how much a particular course of action would reduce a particular sex offender's likelihood of recidivism.

Although numerous efforts are now underway to reduce the likelihood of future offending through active treatment interventions, very few attempts have been made to evaluate treatment outcome by using appropriate scientific methodology (e.g., appropriate control groups, follow-up, measures of recidivism). Hence it is not yet clear what the most appropriate targets of interventions are, and what techniques are best suited to address these targets. It is highly likely that the dynamic variables known to be related to sexual recidivism (e.g., deviant sexual preferences, psychopathic characteristics) are appropriate treatment targets (or, at least, appropriate supervision targets). Some interventions designed to alter deviant preferences have produced short-term positive change, but long-term maintenance and relationship of change to recidivism have not yet been demonstrated (for a review see Quinsey & Earls, 1990). Early treatment attempts with individuals scoring high on psychopathy have largely proven to be unsuccessful (e.g., Rice, Harris, & Cormier, 1992).

Because of the recent focus on dynamic predictors of reoffending in the prediction literature, knowledge regarding treatment targets and successful intervention techniques will likely be obtained in conjunction with knowledge of prediction of sexual reoffending. Once again, this knowledge will mostly be limited by the quality of our research methodology.

❏ Note

1. Calculation of average reconviction rates without weighting by sample size generated similar results.

❏ References

Abel, G. G., Becker, J. V., Mittelman, M., Cunningham-Rathner, J., Rouleau, J. L., & Murphy, W. D. (1987). Self-reported sex crimes of nonincarcerated paraphiliacs. *Journal of Interpersonal Violence, 2*, 3-25.

Andrews, D. A., Zinger, I., Hoge, R. D., Bonta, J., Gendreau, P., & Cullen, F. T. (1990). Does correctional treatment work? A clinically relevant and psychologically informed meta-analysis. *Criminology, 28*, 369-404.

Barbaree, H. E., & Marshall, W. L. (1988). Deviant sexual arousal, offense history, and demographic variables as predictors of reoffense among child molesters. *Behavior Science and the Law, 6*, 267-280.

Christiansen, K. O., Elers-Nielsen, M., Le Maire, L., & Sturup, G. K. (1965). Recidivism among sexual offenders. In K. O. Christiansen (Ed.), *Scandinavian studies in criminology* (Vol. 1, pp. 55-85). London: Tavistock.

Correctional Service of Canada, Research and Statistics Branch. (1991). Everything you wanted to know about Canadian federal sex offenders and more. *Forum on Corrections Research, 3*, 3-6.

Fitch, J. H. (1962). Men convicted of sexual offenses against children: A descriptive follow-up study. *British Journal of Criminology, 3*, 18-37.

Fleiss, J. L. (1973). *Statistical methods for rates and proportions.* New York: John Wiley.

Freund, K., & Blanchard, R. (1989). Phallometric diagnosis of pedophilia. *Journal of Consulting and Clinical Psychology, 57*, 100-105.

Frisbie, L. V. (1969). *Another look at sex offenders in California* (California Mental Health Research Monograph No. 12). Sacramento: California Department of Mental Hygiene.

Frisbie, L. V., & Dondis, E. H. (1965). *Recidivism among treated sex offenders* (California Mental Health Research Monograph No. 5). Sacramento: California Department of Mental Hygiene.

Furby, L., Weinrott, M. R., & Blackshaw, L. (1989). Sex offender recidivism: A review. *Psychological Bulletin, 105,* 3-30.

Gibbens, T.C.N., Soothill, K. L., & Way, C. K. (1978). Sibling and parent-child incest offenders. *British Journal of Criminology, 18,* 40-52.

Gibbens, T.C.N., Soothill, K. L., & Way, C. K. (1981). Sex offenses against young girls: A long-term record study. *Psychological Medicine, 11,* 351-357.

Gottfredson, D. M., Wilkins, L. T., & Hoffman, P. B. (1978). *Guidelines for parole and sentencing: A policy control method.* Lexington, MA: Lexington Books.

Gray, K. C., & Mohr, J. W. (1965). Follow-up of male sexual offenders. In R. Slovenko (Ed.), *Sexual behavior and the law* (pp. 742-756). Springfield, IL: Charles C Thomas.

Greenland, C. (1984). Dangerous sexual offender legislation in Canada, 1948-1977: An experiment that failed. *Canadian Journal of Criminology, 26,* 1-12.

Grunfeld, B., & Noreik, K. (1986). Recidivism among sex offenders: A follow-up study of 541 Norwegian sex offenders. *International Journal of Law and Psychiatry, 9,* 95-102.

Hall, G.C.N., & Proctor, W. C. (1987). Criminological predictors of recidivism in a sexual offender population. *Journal of Consulting and Clinical Psychology, 55,* 111-112.

Hanson, R. K., Steffy, R. A., & Gauthier, R. (1993). Long-term recidivism of child molesters. *Journal of Consulting and Clinical Psychology, 61,* 646-652.

Hare, R. D. (1991). *Manual for the revised Psychopathy Checklist.* Toronto: Multi-Health Systems.

Hare, R. D., & McPherson, L. M. (1984). Violent and aggressive behavior by criminal psychopaths. *International Journal of Law and Psychiatry, 7,* 35-50.

Harris, G. T., Rice, M. E., & Cormier, C. A. (1991). Psychopathy and violent recidivism. *Law and Human Behavior, 15,* 625-632.

Harris, G. T., Rice, M. E., Quinsey, V. L., Chaplin, T. C., & Earls, C. (1992). Maximizing the discriminant validity of phallometric assessment. *Psychological Assessment, 4,* 502-511.

Lalumière, M. L., & Earls, C. M. (1992). Voluntary control of penile responses as a function of stimulus duration and instructions. *Behavioral Assessment, 14,* 121-132.

Lalumière, M. L., & Quinsey, V. L. (1993). The sensitivity of phallometric measures with rapists. *Annals of Sex Research, 6,* 123-138.

Lalumière, M. L., & Quinsey, V. L. (1994). The discriminability of rapists from non-sex offenders using phallometric measures: A meta-analysis. *Criminal Justice and Behavior, 21,* 150-175.

MacCulloch, M. J., Snowden, P. R., Wood, P.J.W., & Mills, H. E. (1983). Sadistic fantasy, sadistic behaviour and offending. *British Journal of Psychiatry, 143,* 20-29.

Marshall, W. L., & Barbaree, H. E. (1990). Outcome of comprehensive cognitive-behavioral treatment programs. In W. L. Marshall, D. R. Laws, & H. E. Barbaree (Eds.), *Handbook of sexual assault: Issues, theories, and treatment of the offender* (pp. 363-385). New York: Plenum.

Nuffield, J. (1982). *Parole decision-making in Canada: Research towards decision guidelines.* Ottawa: Solicitor General Canada.

Pallone, N. J. (1990). *Rehabilitating criminal sexual psychopaths: Legislative mandates, clinical quandaries.* New Brunswick, NJ: Transaction Books.

Quinsey, V. L. (1980). The base-rate problem and the prediction of dangerousness: A reappraisal. *Journal of Psychiatry and Law, 8,* 329-340.

Quinsey, V. L. (1984). Sexual aggression: Studies of offenders against women. In D. N. Weisstub (Ed.), *Law and mental health: International perspectives* (Vol. 1, pp. 84-121). New York: Pergamon.

Quinsey, V. L. (1986). Men who have sex with children. In D. N. Weisstub (Ed.), *Law and mental health: International perspectives* (Vol. 2, pp. 140-172). New York: Pergamon.

Quinsey, V. L., & Ambtman, R. (1979). Variables affecting psychiatrists' and teachers' assessments of the dangerousness of mentally ill offenders. *Journal of Consulting and Clinical Psychology, 47,* 353-362.

Quinsey, V. L., & Chaplin, T. C. (1988a). Penile responses of child molesters and normals to descriptions of encounters with children involving sex and violence. *Journal of Interpersonal Violence, 3,* 259-274.

Quinsey, V. L., & Chaplin, T. C. (1988b). Preventing faking in phallometric assessments of sexual preference. *Annals of the New York Academy of Sciences, 528,* 49-58.

Quinsey, V. L., Chaplin, T. C., & Upfold, D. (1984). Sexual arousal to nonsexual violence and sadomasochistic themes among rapists and non-sex offenders. *Journal of Consulting and Clinical Psychology, 52,* 651-657.

Quinsey, V. L., & Earls, C. M. (1990). The modification of sexual preferences. In W. L. Marshall, D. R. Laws, & H. E. Barbaree (Eds.), *Handbook of sexual assault: Issues, theories, and treatment of the offender* (pp. 279-295). New York: Plenum.

Quinsey, V. L., Harris, G. T., & Rice, M. E. (in press). Actuarial prediction of sexual recidivism. *Journal of Interpersonal Violence.*

Quinsey, V. L., Harris, G. T., Rice, M. E., & Lalumière, M. L. (1993). Assessing treatment efficacy in outcome studies of sex offenders. *Journal of Interpersonal Violence, 8,* 512-523.

Quinsey, V. L., & Lalumière, M. L. (in press). *The assessment of sexual aggressors against children.* Thousand Oaks, CA: Sage.

Quinsey, V. L., & Maguire, A. (1986). Maximum security psychiatric patients: Actuarial and clinical prediction of dangerousness. *Journal of Interpersonal Violence, 1,* 143-171.

Quinsey, V. L., & Walker, W. D. (1992). Dealing with dangerousness: Community risk management strategies with violent offenders. In R. Peters, R. J. McMahon, & V. L. Quinsey (Eds.), *Aggression and violence throughout the lifespan* (pp. 244-262). Newbury Park, CA: Sage.

Radzinowicz, L. (1957). *Sexual offenses: A report of the Cambridge Department of Criminal Science.* New York: Macmillan.

Rice, M. E., Harris, G. T., & Cormier, C. A. (1992). An evaluation of a maximum security therapeutic community for psychopaths and other mentally disordered offenders. *Law and Human Behavior, 16,* 399-412.

Rice, M. E., Harris, G. T., & Quinsey, V. L. (1990). A follow up of rapists assessed in a maximum security psychiatric facility. *Journal of Interpersonal Violence, 5,* 435-448.

Rice, M. E., Quinsey, V. L., & Harris, G. T. (1991). Predicting sexual recidivism among treated and untreated extrafamilial child molesters released from a maximum security psychiatric institution. *Journal of Consulting and Clinical Psychology, 59,* 381-386.

Romero, J. J., & Williams, L. M. (1985). Recidivism among convicted sex offenders: A ten-year follow-up study. *Federal Probation, 49,* 58-64.

Serin, R. C. (1991). Psychopathy and violence in criminals. *Journal of Interpersonal Violence, 6,* 423-431.

Soothill, K. L., Jack, A., & Gibbens, T.C.N. (1976). Rape: A 22-year cohort study. *Medicine, Science, and the Law, 16,* 62-69.

Sturgeon, V. H., & Taylor, J. (1980). Report of a five-year follow-up study of mentally disordered sex offenders released from Atascadero State Hospital in 1973. *Criminal Justice Journal, 4,* 31-63.

Williamson, S., Hare, R. D., & Wong, S. (1987). Violence: Criminal psychopaths and their victims. *Canadian Journal of Behavioural Science, 19,* 454-462.

Wormith, J. S., & Ruhl, M. (1986). Preventive detention in Canada. *Journal of Interpersonal Violence, 1,* 399-430.

Author Index

Subject Index

About the Editor

Jacquelyn C. Campbell, PhD, RN, FAAN, is the Anna D. Wolf Endowed Professor at the Johns Hopkins University School of Nursing. She has been conducting research with battered women, as well as working with shelters and advocacy projects, for the past 15 years.

About the Contributors

Grant T. Harris, PhD, is a Research Psychologist at the Mental Health Centre in Penetanguishene, Ontario. Formerly he was responsible for the development and supervision of behavioral programs on a maximum security unit for dangerous and assaultive men. His research interests include violent and criminal behavior, sexual aggression, psychopathy, psychopharmacology, and decision making.

Martin L. Lalumière received his MPs in clinical psychology from the Université de Montréal in 1990. He is a PhD candidate in forensic psychology at Queen's University, Kingston. He is also a research fellow at the Departments of Psychology and Psychiatry, Queen's University. His research interests include sexual preferences and sexual deviances, delinquency and psychopathy, and mating strategies and evolutionary psychology.

Barbara J. Limandri, DNSc, RN, CS, is Associate Professor at Oregon Health Sciences University, School of Nursing. She is a Psychiatric-Mental Health Nurse Practitioner with clinical emphasis on family violence.

Joel S. Milner, PhD, is currently Professor of Psychology, Presidential Research Professor, and Director of the Family Violence Research

Program at Northern Illinois University. Since 1989 he has been an Associate Editor of *Violence and Victims,* and he recently edited three special issues of *Criminal Justice and Behavior,* each of which focused on a different type of family problem. He has served as ad hoc grant reviewer for NIMH and NCCAN and as a member (1988-1993) and Chair (1990-1993) of the VTS IRG (NIMH). He has published more than 100 articles, chapters, and books, the majority in the area of family violence, and his programmatic research has focused on the description and prediction of physical child abuse and intrafamilial sexual child abuse. Currently this research includes studies on an intrafamilial sexual child abuse screening scale and the testing of a social-information processing model of physical child abuse.

Vernon L. Quinsey received his PhD in experimental psychology from the University of Massachusetts at Amherst. He was first a psychologist and later Director of Research at the maximum security Oak Ridge Division of the Mental Health Centre in Penetanguishene, Ontario. Since 1988 he has been Professor and Coordinator of Forensic/Correctional Studies in the Psychology Department of Queen's University in Kingston. His research interests include violent criminal behavior, sex offending, and evolution and behavior.

Marnie E. Rice, PhD, is the Director of Research at the Mental Health Centre in Penetanguishene, Ontario. She is a psychologist with extensive experience in applications of social learning theory to forensic populations. She has published in the areas of aggression and criminal behavior, social competence, institutional violence, sex offending, arson, and the prediction of violent behavior.

Daniel G. Saunders, MSW, PhD, is Associate Professor at the University of Michigan, School of Social Work, where he teaches courses on methods for preventing domestic violence and conducts research on the topic. His current research is on predictors of post-traumatic stress in battered women and comparisons of different treatments for men who batter. His publications cover the assessment and treatment of men who batter, public and professional attitudes about domestic violence, and battered women's use of violence.

Daniel J. Sheridan, MS, RN, is a doctoral student at Oregon Health Sciences University, School of Nursing, and a Family Violence Consultant at Oregon Health Sciences University Hospital.